SUTTON

PAST & PRESENT

SARA GOODWINS

SUTTON PUBLISHING

Sutton Publishing Limited
Phoenix Mill · Thrupp · Stroud
Gloucestershire · GL5 2BU

First published 2004

Copyright © Sara Goodwins, 2004

British Library Cataloguing in Publication Data
A catalogue record for this book is available from the
British Library.

ISBN 0-7509-3424-7

Typeset in 10.5/13.5 Photina.
Typesetting and origination by
Sutton Publishing Limited.
Printed and bound in England by
J.H. Haynes & Co. Ltd, Sparkford.

Title page photograph: High Street, looking north, 1968. In the 1880s this part of the High Street was known as Cock Hill after the hotel at its top. The High Street is part of the direct route to Brighton and was laid out as a new turnpike road following a much older drover's track. Turnpikes were financed and maintained by tolls and the toll bar would have been just about where the photographer was standing. In fact there were two at that point, one barring the Brighton Road and a second at right angles to it on the Cheam Road, the same toll house serving both. This part of the High Street has been pedestrianised since the 1970s. (*John Puttock*)

For my father.
Deaf. Daft. Cantankerous.
Extraordinarily creative and dearly loved.

St Nicholas' Church, Sutton, 1798. Giles Hatch was rector of St Nicholas' at the time J. Laporte drew this sketch of his church. A decade earlier, on 8 August 1788, a collection was taken at the church of St Martin, Ludgate to help pay for the building of a steeple at Sutton church. The 'steeple' was probably the brick tower shown in the sketch, which replaced the old wooden tower. The Ludgate collection raised 9s 7d of the £600 needed and the sketch might even have been produced to show the Ludgate congregation how and where their donation had been spent. (*Courtesy St Nicholas' Church*)

CONTENTS

Aerial view of Sutton looking north-east, 1972. The tallest building in the photograph, Vigilant House, was completed in 1966 to a very unusual design. The core of the building, where the lifts are, forms a framework from which cantilevers support the offices which are suspended on steel ropes. Until the curtain wall was extended to ground level, the bulk of the building appeared to hover above the ground. Its unusual construction means that the building is very lively in high winds. At the time of the photograph the building was used by Atomic Power Construction Ltd., and it was here that Dungeness B power station was designed. Now called South Point, the building is currently occupied by Kellogg Brown & Root. (*Courtesy of Sutton and East Surrey Water*)

INTRODUCTION

Sutton is old. A community has existed here since the eighth century. In fact archaeological finds go back over ten thousand years, but for most of the town's life it was no bigger than any of its neighbours. The problem was water, or rather the lack of it.

The main geology of the area around Sutton is London clay to the north and chalk to the south. Between the two is a narrow belt of Thanet sand, which runs from St Nicholas' Church to Angel Hill. London clay is not very porous so moisture lingers on the surface and is easily contaminated, while water leaches through chalk as through a sieve. Thanet sand holds water which occasionally emerges as a spring or which can be made available by digging relatively shallow wells. All along this belt of Thanet sand small communities settled to farm the rich arable land and hunt game in the nearby woods and downs. One of those communities became Sutton.

For most of its life the town has been tiny. In 1801 Sutton still only had a population of 579 – about the same number as work in just one of its office blocks today. Sutton was one of a chain of settlements, including Carshalton to the east and Cheam to the west, that were home to agricultural workers deriving most of what they needed from the land. Travellers would have been few, strangers rare and life circumscribed by the seasons. In summer those living in Sutton would have spent most of their time out of doors to take advantage of the warmth and light. In winter they would have huddled inside with their beasts and may have gone hungry.

There has always been rivalry between Sutton and its neighbours, traces of which still remain even today. Many small settlements were founded at roughly the same time and stayed roughly the same size, determined by how many people the land could support. Local feeling was strong and a 'foreigner' was someone who hadn't been born in your village. It was communication by road and rail which first stimulated Sutton's growth and the laying of piped water to its residents which made growth possible. Regular contact with the outside world not only brought expansion but also sophistication. Small businesses sprang up, at first directly related to travellers on the turnpike – bakers and brewers to feed visitors, seamstresses to offer running repairs, leather workers to make or mend harness, etc. – and then to provide trade goods for neighbouring communities. By the time the railway arrived Sutton's people had become travellers themselves and wealthy middle-class families could visit London and the coast relatively easily.

Twelve hundred years after Sutton's acquisition by Chertsey Abbey there could hardly be a greater contrast between the agricultural settlement and the bustling commuter town. Today Sutton is a borough of London, at the heart of local

Harry Gillis, Water Inspector, plus cat, 1910. Water inspectors look for leaks in the miles of underground pipes and test underground mains and services. The Sutton and Cheam Water Company was incorporated on 15 June 1863 and claimed, in its first report issued in December of the same year, that 'pipes are laid down for supplying nearly the whole of the principal inhabitants in Sutton and Cheam with water'. Supply began on 1 January 1864. (*Courtesy of Sutton and East Surrey Water*)

government and responsible for many of its former rivals such as Cheam, Wallington and Carshalton. But this book is not concerned with the local politics and administration of the area, or at least only so far as it affects Sutton town and the people who call it home. Modern Sutton with its thriving businesses, busy shopping centres and huge variety of eateries is still the centre of a community. In an odd way, much of Sutton's trade is still geared towards serving those visiting or just passing through. Perhaps things haven't changed so much after all.

Several memorable books containing some stunning photographs have already been published about Sutton. The author is a great admirer of the collection of excellent photographic material held in the Sutton Heritage Collection by Sutton Library, but has attempted to show a side of Sutton which is perhaps less well documented, using photographs most of which have not previously been seen by the public. If the author has produced something which will add to the history books written about Sutton in the past, and provide a starting point for those which will undoubtedly be written in the future, she will have succeeded. If she has also managed to produce something entertaining along the way, so much the better.

1

Around the Town

An aerial view of chalk pit and Manor Park, looking north-east, 1972. In the top right-hand corner is Sutton Waterworks (see p. 17), while Manor Park House (see p. 13) and the war memorial are clearly visible to the left of the photograph. The war memorial is of Portland stone and was erected in 1921 by public subscription. It was designed by J.S.W. Burmester FRIBA who lived in Grange Road. *(Courtesy of Sutton and East Surrey Water)*

Sutton might be old but for most of its life it has been a relatively small and unimportant hamlet on the edge of the North Downs. Its name derives from the Old English *suð* (south) and *tun* or *tone* (settlement), although Sutton may not have been what it was originally called. Chertsey Abbey was founded in about 666 and certainly in its early years had a reputation for renaming estates and lands it acquired, particularly if the original name was pagan in origin. There is some indication – by no means conclusive – that Sutton was originally known as Thunderfield, meaning 'open land belonging to Thunor or Thor'. Thor was often worshipped outside and there is a strong link between the god and the fertility of the earth. Early settlers may have hallowed the land in Thor's name before building dwellings or sowing their crops.

The centre of the original medieval settlement was further north than it is today and, like its neighbours, was very small. The Domesday Book says: 'there are 2 carucates in the demesne and 29 villeins and 4 cottars with 13 carucates. There are 2 churches and 2 bondmen and 2 acres of meadow. The wood yields 10 swine [sic].' A carucate was an area of land which one plough could till in a year. Cottars and villeins are both ranks of peasant; the former are slightly superior. Domesday was compiled in 1086 and, translated, says that Sutton covered about 800 acres with about 200 inhabitants living in about thirty houses.

Just over 700 years later Sutton hadn't grown much. It still had a population of fewer than 600 people, virtually all of whom were living in the area between St Nicholas' Church and Angel Hill where access to water was easiest. Until the coming of the railway there were only two buildings apart from farms south of St Nicholas' Church: the Cock Hotel and Sutton Court. Sutton Court stood in Carshalton Road roughly where the old police station is and was built by John Martindale who had a stud of horses said to be the finest in Europe. The Cock probably had its origins as a resting place for horses after the long pull up the road which was to become Sutton High Street. As the two establishments were built relatively close to each other and, moreover, had to take care of livestock, it suggests that there must have been a nearby water source, probably a very deep well. If this is the case no trace of it has yet been found.

The name of the Cock Hotel probably originated from the cock horses necessary along this part of the road (see p. 26) and which were stabled further down the High Street. Some sources say that stabling for the cock horses was available at the Greyhound, the other coaching inn in the town, roughly where the northern entrance of the St Nicholas Centre is today. Public houses abound in Sutton; at one stage the Victorian working-class suburb of Newtown had nine. The photographer remembers the New Town Inn being famous for its bacon and mushroom sandwiches about twenty years ago.

Newtown is a fascinating part of Sutton for anyone who likes architecture. The area was planned as terraced housing by Thomas Alcock, Lord of the Manor and must have been just on the edge of the water-retentive Thanet sand as no piped water was yet available. Not only is Newtown relatively unspoilt, it's full of variety. Alcock and later developers were not really interested in the design of working-class housing, having in mind a much grander project: the middle-class development of Benhilton. As a result Newtown grew without what would probably today be called a 'mission statement'. Different builders were responsible for different small plots and the result is a delightful hotchpotch of houses in all sorts of different styles.

There are still quite a lot of pubs in the area, but the most interestingly named has to be the Jenny Lind. A famous singer and the first Professor of Singing at the Royal College of Music, Swedish-born Johanna Maria Lind was visiting friends in Carshalton Road in 1847. To the delight of the crowd the world-famous soprano used her host's balcony to give an impromptu performance of an aria from Verdi's opera *Roberto*. Residents were so enchanted that they named one of the local roads after her. When Harry Clowser built his pub in 1854 he named it after the road – unless he too had been one of the spellbound crowd listening to Jenny Lind sing. The pub has recently been renamed the Nightingale, but even this is not inappropriate. Jenny Lind was popularly known as 'the Swedish Nightingale'.

Until 1864 building in Sutton was constrained by the scarcity of water so, as still frequently happens in the town, large houses were pulled down and their site redeveloped. Sutton Court was an early casualty, as was Camden House which stood on the south side of where Camden Road runs today. It was one of the largest mansions in Sutton and the home of Edward Solly, a Fellow of the Royal Society, well-known antiquary and contributor to historic journals. Many of the mature trees in the area, including the magnificent horse chestnut along Western Road, probably started life in Camden House grounds.

The area's long drought ended on 1 January 1864 when Sutton District Water Company, incorporated on 15 June the previous year, began to supply piped water. Modern Sutton became possible. With a fresh water supply, good connections by road and rail and growing business opportunities for those serving the influx of visitors and residents Sutton began to grow much faster than its near neighbours. The first of the new houses to be built south of the railway was Wellesley Lodge, situated where Copse Hill is today. It was built in 1861 by Robert Montgomery Martin whose father was secretary to Sir Arthur Wellesley, later the Duke of Wellington. More building soon followed this early development. In 1869 there were nine houses in Brighton Road south of the railway; by 1878 there were fifty-five.

Many of the Victorian buildings made possible by the availability of fresh water have themselves been swept away in the huge changes which occurred in the town during the 1960s and '70s and which continue on a smaller scale today. The character of Sutton changed totally when two completely new roads, Throwley Way and St Nicholas Way, were pushed through parallel to and east and west of the High Street to create a ring road. Much of the centre of Sutton is peppered with modern cubes masquerading as architecture but the outskirts still show signs of a more gracious age. One of the town's oldest buildings is on Brighton Road; Sutton Lodge is the Georgian farmhouse of what was Sutton Farm. It is now owned by the council and used as a day centre for the elderly. Sutton Grange, which lay between Mulgrave Road and Worcester Road, has gone but its lodges remain, the largest being in the acute angle of the sharp right-hand bend in Worcester Road. Much has changed in Sutton – not all of it for the best – but buildings from different periods do survive and offer not only a surprising richness of detail but also mute witness to the changing tastes in architecture.

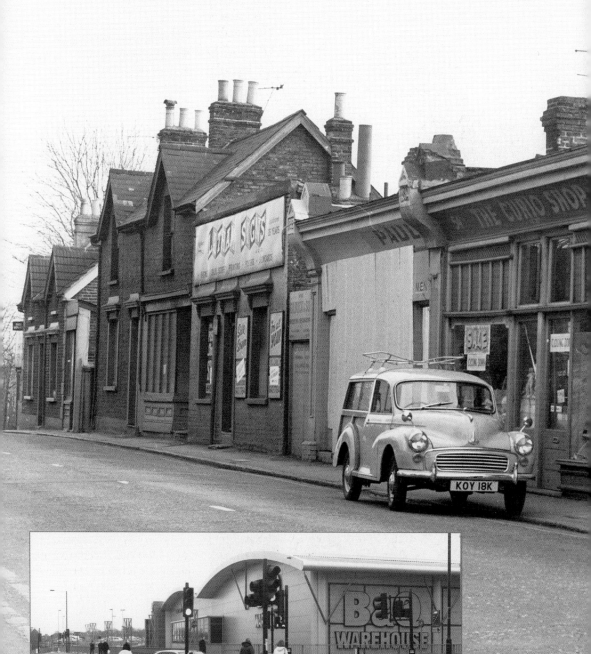

The western end of Carshalton Road, *c.* 1973. The shop in the foreground, Lens of Sutton, was famous to transport enthusiasts all over the country for its range of transport photographs, books and magazines. The name is quite correct without an apostrophe as it refers to the part of the camera and not to the shop's proprietor, John Smith. The Morris Minor estate parked outside the Curio shop next door is only a year or two old. Better known as the 'Traveller', the car, with its ash frame, must be one of the few road vehicles to have been at risk from woodworm. *(Ron Taylor, Cheam Camera Club)*

Inset: The western end of Carshalton Road, 21 February 2004. Apart from the widened road nothing from the previous picture remains. The B&Q Warehouse is the second on the site and was opened in 2002 after being totally rebuilt during the previous two years. The store's design, with its wide travolator suitable for taking shopping trolleys, is a direct result of B&Q expanding into China in 1998. The shortage of land in some Chinese cities forced Kingfisher, the chain's owner, to build some stores on two levels. A similar problem faced the new Sutton store so the oriental solution was installed. *(George Hobbs)*

Manor Park House, Manor Park Road, 1968. The house had been built in 1871 for John Ruck, a wine merchant, who lived there with his wife and six children until his death in 1888. After his wife's death, in 1894, Manor Park House stood empty before being used as Sutton Preparatory School until the First World War, when Sutton Council bought Manor Park House and used it to house Belgian refugees. (John Puttock)

Site of Manor Park House, 7 March 2004. After the First World War six rooms in the house were leased as classrooms and used by Sutton Grammar School (see p. 70). By 1922 a seventh room became available but there was still intense overcrowding. Mr H. Morris, one of the teaching staff and Second Master (deputy head) from 1934, commented: 'Classes occupied what had been the dining room, sitting room and bedroom: some over-flowed to the "tin tabernacle" [an old tin army hut used as a work-shop] and the stables. One of the Sixth Forms occupied an attic at the top of some sixty stairs.' From 1937 the old building housed Sutton Public Library but was demolished in 1976. (George Hobbs)

Opposite, above: Rear elevation of 48–58 Carshalton Road, 18 May 1950. This picture shows the rear of the row of shops which included Lens of Sutton (see previous page) and demonstrates clearly why B&Q was able to be built on two storeys. The chalk pit was owned by the Sutton District Water Company and called Langley Park Lagoon, in which precipitated chalk from the water-softening process was stored. The bank visible in front of the buildings was to protect them from chalk sludge, while the white-banded posts marked the boundary line. *(Courtesy of Sutton and East Surrey Water)*

Left: Langley Park Lagoon, facing west, 18 May 1950. The tattiness and general desolation make it difficult to realise that at the beginning of the twentieth century the council wanted to lease the chalk pit and turn it into pleasure gardens. The *Sutton and Epsom Advertiser* of 17 January 1908 describes the pit as 'a picturesque spot with rugged sides covered with shrubs. At the bottom is a pool of water, and on the east a shelving plot of ground is covered with fruit trees and garden produce.' A plan to turn the pit into an arboretum was thought to be too ambitious but Councillor Wootten spoke for many when he said that he was 'more than disappointed' that the scheme had failed to be realised. *(Courtesy of Sutton and East Surrey Water)*

Paying the water rates, *c*. 1950. Sammy Woods and Eric Clarke are in the payment office which was on the site of what is now B&Q. Sutton is unusual in that its water is still supplied by an independent company pumping water from bore holes in the chalk. Climate changes mean that less rain is falling to replace depleted underground stocks. Between January and October 2003 the south-east received only two-thirds of the usual amount of rainfall, with August and September being the driest period since records began in 1873. *(Courtesy of Sutton and East Surrey Water)*

Langley Park Road, 1982. These four houses were owned by the water company and reserved for the use of company employees. They were demolished in August 1982. Langley Park Road was known as Goodenough's Lane until the 1870s and the chalk pit where B&Q now stands was called Goodenough's Pit. Both were named after local landowner William Goodenough, who lived in the pit with his wife and three daughters until the 1840s. *(Courtesy of Sutton and East Surrey Water)*

Langley Park Road, 21 February 2004. Although the huge ramp to the B&Q car park has not improved the view for the local residents it's good to see that the trees still exist. The B&Q car park may not look very pretty but it has won an award. The Campaign for Dark Skies, an organisation lobbying to reduce the light pollution which prevents stars being visible in the night sky, presented B&Q with a Good Lighting Award. The store was commended for installing cut-off lights in its car park. *(George Hobbs)*

The Elms, *c.* 1950. There's some debate about whether The Elms was built about 1820 or in about 1860. The latter seems more likely as it was the accommodation provided by the Sutton District Water Company (incorporated in 1864) for the manager of Sutton Waterworks. The house had extensive grounds including two ornate fountains and was actually on the site of the waterworks. Its entrance was along a 200ft drive from Carshalton Road, opposite and just west of where Reading Road is today. *(Courtesy of Sutton and East Surrey Water)*

Below: The Elms, early 1980. The Victorian manager's house was replaced by a more modern building in 1961, which was itself demolished in 1980. The 1961 summer was particularly dry and Sutton residents were urged not to waste water. Consumption of water rose to 18.2 million gallons in July 1961 easily beating the 1959 record of 17 million gallons. Pleas for economy carried no weight with some people, however. Writing to the *Daily Telegraph* on 3 September 1961, Mr W.J. Kilpatrick of nearby Oxted said: 'Cheap water my foot! With a climate like ours we should be paid to consume the stuff.' *(Courtesy of Sutton and East Surrey Water)*

Sutton waterworks looking east, 23 May 1964. The pumping station and treatment plant were built in 1903 after an Act of Parliament required the company to soften the water it supplied to a hardness not exceeding nine grains per gallon (gpg). Hardness is caused by minerals, particularly calcium and magnesium, absorbed into the water as it travels through the ground. Hardness is generally measured in grains per gallon: 1gpg being slightly hard; 10 gpg very hard. 1963 was the water company's centenary and much publicity was given to the fact that the steam-driven pumping works at Sutton were being upgraded to new pumping units powered by diesel and electricity. *(Courtesy of Sutton and East Surrey Water)*

Below: Turnpike Lane looking east, 7 March 2004. Sutton waterworks was demolished in August 1985 when the company moved to more modern premises in Gander Green Lane (see p. 46–7). A modern housing development was built instead but the connection with the water company is not quite lost. The area is known as the Water Gardens estate. *(George Hobbs)*

Sutton waterworks looking north-east, April 1980. Slightly below the centre of the picture is The Elms (see p. 16) in the process of being demolished. Conspicuous to the left of The Elms are the lime-water tanks, part of the water-softening process, which cost around £60,000 when they were installed in 1904. In the bottom right-hand corner are the four semi-detached houses in Langley Park Road (see p. 15). The white building in the centre of the photo-graph above The Elms is the New Town Inn (see Introduction, p. 8). It was built in 1870 and took its name from the area which began to develop rapidly around the middle of the nineteenth century. Just visible in the top left corner is the warehouse belonging to Amos Reynolds, cabinet maker, removal firm and undertaker. (Courtesy of Sutton and East Surrey Water)

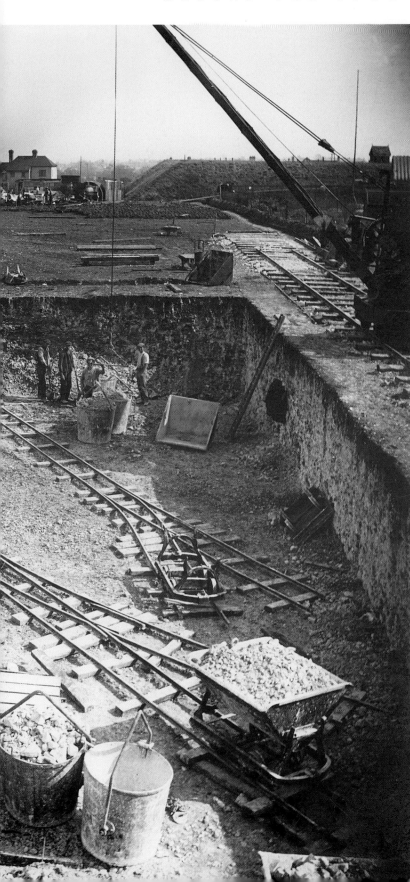

Construction of Langley Park Reservoir, March 1928. This view looks north-east; the houses to the left are in Chalgrove Road, the further ones in the centre in Upland Road. One reservoir capable of holding 1 million gallons of drinking water had already been built on the site and is visible in the top right-hand corner. At the beginning of the First World War there was concern that enemy agents might poison the water supply. The original Langley Park Reservoir and the ten other reservoirs and water towers belonging to the water company were guarded day and night by employees to ensure, as a local paper put it, 'residents a continuation of the ample supply of pure water to which they have become accustomed'. *(Courtesy of Sutton and East Surrey Water)*

Construction of Langley Park Reservoir, 24 August 1928. Without the tiny figure of the man there would be nothing to show the sheer scale of the columns designed to support the cover for the reservoir. Facilities at Sutton waterworks were considered so modern that on 8 September 1931 the Sutton District Water Company welcomed the Directors and Commissaires of the Inter-communale Company, Antwerpshe Water-werken, for an educational tour of inspection. At the luncheon provided, one of the Sutton Water Company's Directors, Sir Edward J. Holland, High Sheriff and Deputy Lieutenant of the County, caused international amusement by commenting that water had been conspicuous by its absence. *(Courtesy of Sutton and East Surrey Water)*

Langley Park Reservoir, 15 June 2003. The view shows the pumping house and is taken from Upland Road looking west. As housing stock increases and the demand for water grows summers are becoming hotter and drier. It's estimated that by 2020 summers will be an average of one degree hotter than now. It doesn't sound much but the present climate is only five degrees warmer than it was in the last ice age! *(George Hobbs)*

Tithe barn, Sutton, *c*. 1935. Originally tithes were an agreed proportion, usually but not invariably one-tenth, paid out of the yearly profits of cultivation or farming to support the church and clergy. As Sutton was and is a rectory, the rector would have been entitled to collect what were called 'great tithes', usually corn, grain, hay and wood. A vicar would commonly have only been entitled to collect 'small tithes' which could include milk, eggs, wool, fish, etc. A tithe barn would therefore be necessary for a rector but not usually for a vicar. An old Surrey farm account book for 1850 reveals the problems such huge storage areas had with vermin; the rat catcher was paid 1*d* per dozen rats killed. The Sutton tithe barn was demolished in the early years of the Second World War so that garages could be built on the site. *(Courtesy St Nicholas' Church)*

St Nicholas' Community Hall and rectory, 7 March 2004. The photograph is not quite on the same alignment as the one above, as the large door in the side of the old barn would have been roughly where the car is in the centre of the photograph. The rectory is the building with the skylights in the roof and although not quite as grand as the building it replaces (see p. 32) is still very handy for St Nicholas' Church. *(George Hobbs)*

Sutton Heritage Mosaic, work in progress, 1994. Commissioned by the London Borough of Sutton to enhance the new Town Square development, the mosaic was funded by Appledown Properties Ltd. The mosaic was made using the reverse technique which allowed it to be made in a studio. A full size outline or cartoon of the design is drawn in reverse on to paper. Here Gary Drostle is fitting the individual tiles within the outlines of the paper design and sticking them down using flour and water glue. Just under Gary's right hand is a depiction of the draft horse pulling trucks along the first iron railway which ran beside the River Wandle. (Courtesy Gary Drostle)

Sutton Heritage Mosaic, work in progress, 1994. Once the tesserae are formed into pictures and patterns and stuck to the reverse of the paper the mosaic can be divided into manageable sections and stuck to a surface – in this case a vertical wall. Here Rob Turner is working on scaffolding about 30ft off the ground laying the cement bed for the next mosaic section. The horse under Gary's hand in the top photograph can be seen near Rob's head. It is facing the other way as the tesserae of that section have now been cemented to the wall. (Courtesy Gary Drostle)

Sutton Heritage Mosaic, work in progress, 1994. Mosaic artists Gary Drostle and Rob Turner were given the brief to depict some of Sutton's heritage and presented the borough's Public Arts Committee with half a dozen designs. The committee chose a design incorporating a classical geometric pattern with nineteen panels each depicting a different aspect of local history; the artists still own the copyright of the design. The tesserae-covered paper sections were reassembled on the wall, the paper was washed off with water and the mosaic grouted and polished. *(Courtesy Gary Drostle)*

Sutton Heritage Mosaic, 1994. The mosaic measures 5m × 7m and is constructed from 20mm² vitreous ceramic tesserae (small tiles made of glass and clay). Consisting of well over 100,000 pieces the mosaic took over 1,500 hours to design and construct. The completed mosaic makes a fitting background to the artists Gary Drostle (left) and Rob Turner, and the Mayor of Sutton. The mayor for the session 1993–4 was Frank Sharp, for 1994–5 Sheila Siggins, so presumably this is Mr Sharp. *(Courtesy Gary Drostle)*

The Cock Hotel, 1894. As the hotel is at the top of a steep hill, the 'cock' in question probably referred originally to a cock horse. Such horses were hitched to the front of the regular team at the bottom of a steep hill, helped haul the load up the incline and were then unhitched at the top. A cock horse was used in Sutton High Street until about 1885. The London to Brighton stagecoach began in 1760 and the Cock Hotel was the 9 a.m. breakfast stop for coaches leaving the City two hours earlier. Almost 250 years later it still takes about two hours to travel from the City to Sutton. *(Courtesy Pearson Cycle Specialists)*

Cock crossroads, 31 March 2004. Although the hotel itself has been demolished, the inn sign – depicting a rooster rather than a horse – still remains just off to the left of this view. The Cock Hotel pictured at the top of the page was the second of that name and occupied the site of the building with the small dome in the picture below. The third Cock Hotel, built around 1900, was erected in front of the building it superseded, probably to ensure no loss of trade. It was demolished around 1963 but occupied the position now taken by Old Inn House and is the reason for the stepped frontage. *(George Hobbs)*

The Railway Tavern, 1885. The wooden pillar and archway spanning the street is the other end of the beam supporting the sign for the Cock Hotel (out of view to the left). In the nineteenth century purveyors of pork were licensed separately from other butchers. George Watts probably kept a few pigs fattened on scraps from his own fruit and vegetable shop and possibly eked out by the leftovers from his neighbour's brewing and Mr Anscomb's bakery business. No doubt bacon was gratefully received in return. *(Courtesy Pearson Cycle Specialists)*

Long Island, O'Neills, 2 April 2004. The Railway Tavern was renamed the Green Man which name the pub retained until very recently when it became O'Neill's. There are several versions of the origin of the name the Green Man. The more prosaic is that the landlord always wore a green apron but one version has it that one of the licensees was so warm-hearted when it came to granting credit that people took advantage of his kindness and referred to him as a 'green man'. *(George Hobbs)*

Left: Cock crossroads, 1959. The third Cock Hotel (see p. 26) is visible on the right while on the left is William Pile Ltd, bookseller, stationer and printer. The clock on the roof of the building had the reputation of being the most accurate in the town. Pile's closed in 1966 and became the electricity board showrooms. The bus displays the route number 725 and was the only orbital route on London's famous Green Line limited stop services; all the others radiated outwards from central London. The 725 route began on 1 July 1953 and operated between Windsor and Gravesend, serving Staines, Kingston, Sutton, Croydon, Bromley and Dartford. Heathrow Airport was obviously not a traffic objective in those days! (© *Alan Cross*)

Below left: Cock crossroads, 31 March 2004. The building which housed Pile's was demolished in 1987, 104 years after it was built, and replaced by a red-brick four-storey office building. With a frontage on the High Street it seems odd that no retail outlet was built. Most of the High Street is now pedestrianised but the one-way system allows eastbound traffic through to Carshalton Road at this point. (*George Hobbs*)

Above right: Pedestrian underpass, 21 December 2003. Sutton Council purchased Sutton Public Hall in 1920 and it was regularly used for exhibitions, dances and various social events. A number of well-known entertainers including Noel Coward, Leslie Howard and Jack Warner performed there. The Public Hall was demolished in 1981. Presumably somebody thought the brick and glass monstrosity which is Chancery House to be an improvement on the old building. Note that the retaining wall of the underpass has had to be reinforced by additional buttressing. (*George Hobbs*)

Right: Sutton Public Hall, *c*. 1980. The photograph is unusual in that it shows the new pedestrian underpass as well as the Public Hall. Sutton Public Hall was built as a private venture in 1878 and rooms leased to whoever wanted to use them. Until the building of the municipal offices (see p. 30) the local authority rented a number of the Hall's ancillary rooms. In 1913, Sutton County School, later called Sutton Grammar School, arranged to use two rooms in Sutton Public Hall as overspill classrooms. The Hall's nickname – 'The Pub' – was hilariously misconstrued by one shocked school inspector, until he was hastily corrected. (*John Puttock*)

Sutton Municipal Offices, 1968. Built in 1900 on the site of a chalk pit and brick and flint cottage, the municipal offices celebrated Sutton's new status as an Urban District Council, granted in 1894. Sutton had been growing much more quickly than its near neighbours, largely because of the new toll road to Brighton laid in 1755; the coaching inns required both staff and nearby provision merchants. In 1801 Cheam was slightly larger than Sutton with a population of 616 to Sutton's 579. One century later Cheam's population was 3,404 while Sutton's had risen to 17,223. Road transport began Sutton's growth and the coming of the railways accelerated it. Sutton Municipal Offices cost £8,372 to build and reflected the town's civic pride. *(John Puttock)*

Surrey House, 21 December 2003. One wonders what Sutton Council was thinking of. Sutton Municipal Offices were demolished in 1971 and this modern combination of store and offices built in 1975. At one stage occupied by the furniture department of Allders, today the building is occupied by Wilkinson. The firm was founded in 1930 in Leicester by J.K. Wilkinson and remains a family-owned business. It now has 232 stores employing 18,000 staff. *(George Hobbs)*

Building of St Nicholas' Centre, c. 1985. The new shopping centre was built behind the High Street, largely on a car park, with its two entrances utilising the existing roads George Street and West Street (see p. 90). George Street was named after George Barnes, a well-known veterinary surgeon, blacksmith and ironmonger who also counted gas-fitting and bell-hanging among his skills. *(Courtesy Robin Hood Junior School)*

St Nicholas' Centre, 7 March 2004. The centre includes seventy-five stores, three restaurants and a UCI multiscreen cinema but does loom rather over Robin Hood Junior School. On the other side of the fence is being erected the controversial £600,000 bus shelter. Transport for London and Sutton Council – in other words taxpayers – jointly funded the shelter which took longer to build than the new Asda superstore erected further down the High Street. The structure might be state of the art with an innovative lighting system but passengers still get wet when it rains. *(George Hobbs)*

Design for St Nicholas' rectory, 29 June 1887. Several designs were suggested (see pp. 124–5) by the architects E.T. Perrott and R.L. Cole but this was the one eventually built. This is the rear of the rectory, viewed from what became the kitchen garden and the side which would have faced the church to the south. Herbert William Turner was appointed rector on 7 February 1886 and either he or the church patron, Hertford College, Oxford, obviously felt that he deserved a new rectory. The disruption to family life was minimised by building the new rectory in the grounds of the old one. He and his wife Ellen had nine children so his home had to be fairly roomy. *(Courtesy St Nicholas' Church)*

8–17 Beech Tree Place, 21 December 2003. There was only a gate for pedestrians to enter the rectory grounds from the east, but the site of the building must have been about here. The rectory shared the fate of many Sutton landmarks when it was demolished to make way for the town's traffic scheme in the early 1970s. Note the carved statues affixed to the wall on the far left and right of the photograph. They are eagles and stood sentinel on top of the two rectory gate-posts in West Street. *(George Hobbs)*

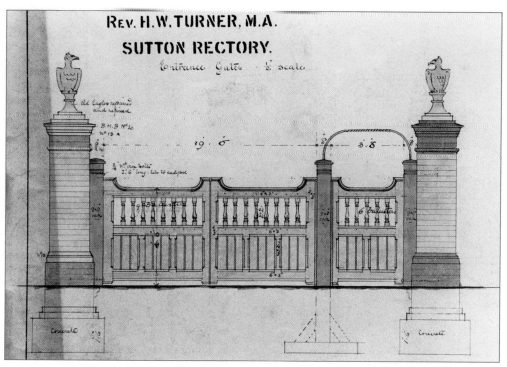

Design for the entrance gate for St Nicholas' rectory, June 1887. The rectory was north of the church and had a drive approximately 100 yards long. Its imposing gates stood in West Street just east of West Street School (see p. 90) and on the opposite side of the road. *(Courtesy St Nicholas' Church)*

Left: Design for the entrance gate for St Nicholas' rectory, detail of eagle, June 1887. Although the entrance gates were new, notes on the plans say 'old eagles to be repaired and refixed' indicating that they were reused from an earlier building, possibly the gates of the previous rectory. *(Courtesy St Nicholas' Church)*

Right: Eagle, 17 Beech Tree Place, 21 December 2004. Although looking a bit battered after more than 120 years in the open air, the eagle is still recognisably one of those which adorned the rectory entrance post. It's seen a lot of changes. *(George Hobbs)*

High Street, looking south, 1968. On the right is Shinner's department store and almost opposite it, Sutton Municipal Offices (see p. 30). In 1899 Ernest Shinner opened his first shop at 79 High Street and gradually extended into all the shops in the terrace but one. The whole of the building is clad in faïence tiles but the extension is marked by the step in the roof line visible in the top right of the photograph. The interior of the shop must have been a nightmare for the staff as it was a homely confusion of different levels and adjoining rooms. (*John Puttock*)

High Street, looking south, 2 April 2004. The presence of a Ferris wheel doesn't indicate carnival time in Sutton; the wheel is a fixture – if a moving one – in the High Street. The first Ferris wheel opened in 1893 in Chicago and was designed by George Ferris to outdo the Eiffel Tower. Sixty riders per car travelled around a wheel 250ft in diameter. Sutton's wheel is a little more modest. (*George Hobbs*)

Right: Policemen going to their beat, in the High Street, approaching the Cock Hotel, 1908. At this time the police station was on the east side of the High Street roughly where W.H. Smith is now. John Redwood (see p. 50) is in the foreground on the right. He took No. 5 Beat Day Duty and wrote it out so that he would not forget it: 'Commencing at the corner of Park Lane and Ewell Road, along Ewell Road to Nonsuch Park, through Nonsuch Park Avenue, Cheam and Ewell Footpath & Ewell Park to Ewell Road by left to Gipsy Lane, and back to Station Road, by left to Railway Station and back to Ewell Road, by left to Monger Lane, by left to Reigate Road, <u>by left</u> to Fir Tree Road, by left to Banstead Railway Station (Gipsy Lane) by left to Ewell Road, by right along Ewell Road to Park Lane & Post, Distance 9 miles 800 Yards; Time 3 Hours, 45 minutes [sic]'. Phew! *(Stephen & Sue Waters)*

Below: Sutton Police Station, 31 March 2004. In 1909 the High Street building was vacated and the police station moved to its current site in Carshalton Road. The original building, closest to the camera, was erected on the site of Sutton Court and is now a Grade II listed building. The massive new extension was officially opened by the commissioner of the Metropolitan Police, Sir John Stevens, on 23 March 2004 although it had been in use for over a year. The new building houses Sutton CID, the criminal justice unit and the borough intelligence unit as well as having thirty cells in a custody suite. *(George Hobbs)*

Left: Sutton Arcade, 1977. The arcade is decorated with flags for the Queen's silver jubilee but might just as well have been celebrating its own golden jubilee. It was built in 1927 by Ernest Shinner (see p. 34). Arcades – covered pedestrian shopping alleys – were first developed in Paris in the late eighteenth century to provide dry, safe shopping away from the dirt and traffic of the roads. The idea was adopted with enthusiasm in Britain, perhaps because the British weather tends to be very much wetter than in continental Europe. Sutton arcade was really the town's first multi-purpose shopping centre. *(Stephen Waters)*

Below left: Virgin megastore, 31 March 2004. Only the back arch remains of the Sutton Arcade but this is where it was. Ever wondered where Virgin name comes from? Richard Branson's Virgin empire began with Virgin Records which he set up in 1970 when he was the 17-year-old student publisher of *Student Magazine.* He needed a name and had almost decided on 'Slipped Disc' when one of the girls in the *Student Magazine* office said, 'What about Virgin? We're complete virgins at business!' Branson liked it and the rest, as they say, is history. Just as well: Slipped Disc might have worked for records, but a railway company? Oh, I don't know though . . . *(George Hobbs)*

Above right: Sutton High Street, *c.* 1860. The tree is roughly where the northern entrance to the St Nicholas' Centre is now. Just before it on the left is the draper's shop owned by Mr Edward Sell and where he lived with his wife and three children. Mr Sell was for a time responsible for collecting the poor rate and overseeing its use for the support of the very poor. The gentleman on the right with arms akimbo and wearing a leather apron was the local village blacksmith, Tom Pearson. He is standing outside his premises, which are now a cycle shop owned and run by his great-great-grandsons (see p. 39). *(Courtesy Pearson Cycle Specialists)*

Right: Sutton High Street, *c.* 1900. The nameboard above the first shop on the right reads 'T. PEARSON Farrier' while the hanging sign says 'H. PEARSON Cycle Agent'. Harry Pearson, one of Tom's sons and a blacksmith by trade, visualised a great future for the pedal cycle and began making them in about 1890. Opposite are the three balls hanging outside Herrington's shop, which combined selling clothing with the business of pawnbroker. A story is told about how the manager of the clothing shop noticed a pair of boots in pawn and asked why they'd been moved there from the display he'd put out that morning. On being told that they'd been taken in pawn, both managers realised that a thief had taken them from the front of the shop straight into the pawn shop. After that incident the boots were chained down! *(Courtesy Pearson Cycle Specialists)*

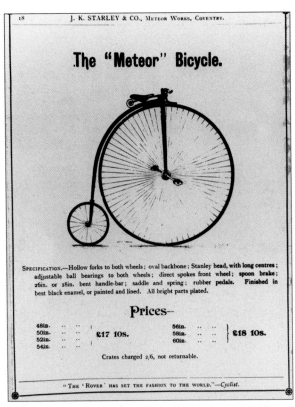

Advert for the Meteor bicycle, 1889. As well as making 'ordinaries', the official name for what became known colloquially as 'penny farthings', John Kemp Starley introduced the 'Rover' bicycle with triangulated frame, chain and gears attached to the rear wheel. The Rover, which first appeared in 1885, is the direct forerunner to the modern safety bicycle. J.K. Starley went on to form the Rover car company – not the only cyclist to transfer his interest to motor transport. On 29 June 1905 defectors from the Cyclist Touring Club (CTC) met at the Trocadero restaurant in London and formed the Automobile Association (the AA). (*Courtesy Pearson Cycle Specialists*)

Williams clock, interior of Pearson cycle shop, 2 April 2004. An alternative application of bicycle chainwheels and cranks, the clock reminds cyclists of the Eddywilly adverts for bicycle components made by the Edward Williams Manufacturing Co. Eddywilly was an amiable and aged gentleman with flat cap and clay pipe who appeared in Heath Robinsonesque cartoons placidly cycling outlandish contraptions. The cartoons were collected and published by John Pinkerton (1934–2002), cyclist, writer and cycling historian. Unlike Eddywilly's mechanical contrivances the Williams clock works and keeps remarkably good time. (*George Hobbs*)

Pearson cycle shop, High Street, 1974. During the 1930s and '40s Sutton half-day closing used to be adhered to rigidly at 1 p.m. on Wednesday – and with good reason. The tradespeople of Sutton High Street ran a cricket side called the Sutton Wednesdays. Arthur Pearson, grandson of the founder and grandfather of the present owners, remembered scoring 99 – his highest score – one Wednesday afternoon in 1935. He also recalled himself and his brother Len fire-watching from the roof of the shop during the Second World War. The log book entry for Saturday 7 June 1941 says: 'All clear. Hitler Windy' [sic]! (Courtesy Pearson Cycle Specialists)

Pearson cycle shop, High Street, 2 April 2004. The current owners, Guy (left) and his brother William Pearson took over the full-time running of the shop in 1997, the fifth generation to do so. Guy is wearing the official Pearson racing strip in blue with yellow lettering. The carbon-fibre framed road-racing bike the brothers are holding is worth rather more than the author's car. Pearson is the only privately owned shop remaining in the High Street and still caters for specialist customers, selling high-specification cycles and equipment as well as catering for high street sales. (George Hobbs)

High Street, looking north, 31 January 1959. The battery electric milk float is from the South Suburban Co-operative Society while the trolleybus is on route 654 to Crystal Palace. The post office is on the corner of the High Street and Benhill Street (now Benhill Avenue) and used to be occupied by Henry Stevens' butcher's shop. There was a small slaughter-house at the rear of the shop and cattle were regularly driven to it down the High Street from one of the outlying farms. (© *A.D. Packer*)

High Street, looking north, 4 October 2003. The High Street is now pedestrianised for much of its length, although bus route 154, successor to the trolleybus, still enters the High Street via Benhill Avenue, doglegs past the building which once housed the post office and turns left to join St Nicholas Way. The lower part of the High Street is often given over to specialist markets such as farmers' markets and occasional stallholders visiting from France. (*George Hobbs*)

Grove Road, *c.* 1954. Bus route 213 usually ran along Cheam Road but on the occasions when road works denied access west-bound services were diverted via Grove Road. The temporary bus stop is outside the telephone exchange, which was built in 1929. When telephone connections were a matter of calling the operator two of the local exchanges were Vigilant and Melville; the nomenclature is still carried on in several local businesses today. In 1959 parking was still permitted in the centre of this part of Grove Road (on the lighter coloured tarmac, bottom left). This section of Grove Road is now part of the busy one-way system. (© *Alan Cross*)

Grove Road, 31 March 2004. Considering all the changes which have been wrought on Sutton elsewhere, the buildings along this section of Grove Road have changed remarkably little. Although not visible from the photograph above, two additional storeys have been added to the telephone exchange and it has sprouted a large number of mobile phone masts – appropriately enough in this case. The post office, although extensively remodelled, has been on this site since 1907 when it moved from 14 High Street. (*George Hobbs*)

Above: Haddon Road looking east, 1977. The road is decorated for the Queen's Silver Jubilee. In the early part of the nineteenth century the north side of Haddon Road, to the left in this picture, contained Thomas Till's livery stables and the Leyton timberyard as well as terraced housing. On 23 September 1923 fire broke out in the timberyard and spread to the houses. The fire station at the time was in the High Street, roughly where the Möben/Dolphin shop is now, and the men and fire pump were on hand within minutes. Even so the fire raged for several hours and extra help was needed from the Carshalton fire brigade. *(Stephen Waters)*

Below: Haddon Road, looking east, 31 March 2004. Built at a cost of £34 million, Asda opened in November 2003. The chain is now part of Wal-Mart but was founded in 1965 by a group of Yorkshire farmers as *Associated Dairies* and still tries to offer products supplied by people and businesses local to each store. The chain is not without a sense of humour. On 15 December 2003 the company issued a press release stating that Longwell Green, a small suburb in Bristol, was the sprout-eating capital of Britain as, in the run up to Christmas, shoppers bought the equivalent of eighty-five sprouts per head of population per week. *(George Hobbs)*

Above: Benhill Street (now Avenue), 21 August 1935. This was the terminus where trams on the Sutton route turned round. Both trams are operated by London Transport but the open-topped tram in the background came from the South Metropolitan Electric Tramways company whereas an ex-London United Tram (LUT) is visible in the foreground. Ex-LUT trams only ran on the Sutton route in the final few years of its existence before being replaced by trolley buses; the second wire needed for trolley buses is already in place. The Grapes public house is behind the car on the left and has gone through several changes of name but is always referred to as The Grapes in the bus timetables. (© *A.D. Packer*)

Below: Benhill Avenue, 4 October 2003. Heading away from the camera is a 1967-registered, Austin A40. This road once formed the northern boundary of Sutton Manor, which is the reason for its curve northwards. It gets its name from Benhill Farm, the farmhouse of which stood on the corner of Benhill Avenue and what is now Throwley Way. It was once the largest farm in Sutton and presumably gave its name to the Victorian suburb Benhilton. (*George Hobbs*)

Angel Bridge, *c.* 1890. The bridge and hill take their name from the Angel Inn, an early nineteenth-century coaching inn at the top of the hill. All sorts of stories abound about why the cutting was dug, including that it was by order of two kings; either Henry VIII wanted to ease his journey to Nonsuch Palace, or the Prince Regent, later George IV, wanted to save his horses at the end of the first stage of his journey to Brighton. The bridge itself is a Victorian footbridge and leads from Sutton Common Road almost to the door of All Saints' Church. The church was completed in 1866 so the bridge may have been built then. *(Author's collection)*

Angel Bridge, 4 October 2003. This is the fourth bridge to be built at Angel Hill. The Victorian structure developed a crack in one of its brick supports and was demolished in 1937. Its replacement, a steel girder bridge, was destroyed by a bomb in September 1940 and was itself replaced by a similar 'temporary' bridge. Forty years later the temporary bridge was removed and the current concrete structure was built when the cutting was lined with imitation stone. The sign on the bridge railings, facing away from the camera, welcomes motorists to Sutton. Signs on the earlier Victorian bridge were more prosaic. They stated baldly: 'BUS PASSENGERS, LOW BRIDGE, REMAIN SEATED.' Ouch! *(George Hobbs)*

Angel Hill looking south, *c.* 1890. Most of this area was owned by Thomas St Leger Alcock who became Lord of the Manor in 1845; Sutton Manor House stood about where Sutton Grammar School stands today. When the railway arrived in Sutton in 1847 and the town quickly began to grow, Alcock became a property developer, laying out Benhill Road (part of which is now All Saints Road), Benhill Street and Benhill Wood Road. He also reserved the land to the left of this photograph for the building of large houses for the well-to-do middle classes. (*Author's collection*)

Angel Hill looking south, 4 October 2003. Sutton Green in the middle distance was preserved by the Sutton Common Enclosure Award of 1810, which appropriated the rest of the parish common land for agriculture. A popular jingle from the time encapsulated public opinion: 'They rightly brand the culprit "thief" / Who steals the goose from off the heath, / But turn the greater felon loose / Who steals the common from the goose.' The Act of Parliament was almost certainly unfair then, but now works to the locals' advantage. Land for building is much sought after in Sutton, but another Act of Parliament would be necessary before building would be allowed on the Green. (*George Hobbs*)

Left: Building new treatment works, Gander Green Lane, looking westwards, July 1975. Modern up-to-date premises and equipment are essential to maintain a good supply of clean water. Built in the late 1970s the treatment works at Gander Green Lane is now half-way through being upgraded and refurbished at a cost of £5½ million. Current works capacity is 14 million gallons per day but once the work is complete this should rise to a possible daily supply of 20 million gallons. *(Courtesy of Sutton and East Surrey Water)*

Inset: Building new treatment works, Gander Green Lane, looking eastwards, 27 May 1977. Gander Green Lane is the road running north (left) to south (right) along the top of the picture. The sharp left-hand bend visible travelling southwards was caused originally by the road skirting the grounds of Lower Cheam House. A small row of shops on that corner on the left is built just about on the site of Cheamhall farmhouse. From there a footpath led due east almost directly to the tithe barn near St Nicholas' Church (see p. 23). *(Courtesy of Sutton and East Surrey Water)*

Gander Green Lane, looking north, *c.* 1930. Only thirty years previously this was a tree-lined lane between fields. It had roadside ponds and wide grass verges along which geese were driven to market, from which it got its name. The tall column on the left-hand pavement is neither a street light nor a telegraph pole but a vent to let noxious fumes escape from the sewers. Several of them are still visible around the area. *(Lilian Curd)*

Gander Green Lane, junction with Elmbrook Road, looking north, 15 June 2003. It's no surprise that there's more traffic in seventy years, but there are also far more trees. Sutton has a tree as its logo and many of its roads are tree-lined. It is considered the greenest of all London boroughs with as many as 500 different species of tree. There are at least five in this photograph alone. *(George Hobbs)*

Ringstead Road, 31 January 1959. It's not clear why the trolleybus conductor is using his bamboo pole to replace the trolley on the wire but his driver may have de-wired by accident. Ringstead Road had been part of the tram route and was widened when track was being laid. Behind the bus on the corner is the Sutton Model Laundry with its huge extractors on the roof. Such an impressive edifice would startle the owners of the first Laundromat, which opened in California in 1851. It was run jointly by a gold miner and a carpenter, had the capacity to wash twelve shirts at a time and was powered by ten donkeys. The mind boggles! *(© A.D. Packer)*

Ringstead Road, 21 December 2003. The road priorities have changed and where the trolley bus used to have right of way to swing left into Westmead Road there is now a cross-roads. The laundry building still stands and is now called Westmead House. It is part of the group of serviced offices which includes Airport House, the former administrative building attached to Croydon airport. Westmead House contains sixty office suites and twenty self-contained business units. *(George Hobbs)*

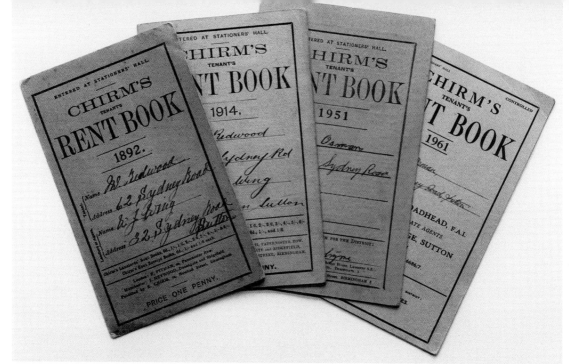

Above: Rent books for 62 Sydney Road. In 1892, when a working man might be paid about 20s per week, the rent was 3s 6d; by 1961, when a reasonable week's pay was about £20, the rent was a mere £1. A general reduction of rents in real terms was in part the result of the Rent and Mortgage Interest Restrictions Act of 1945. It was a mixed blessing; bad landlords were prevented from fleecing their tenants, but good landlords felt discouraged from renting their properties. The number of rented properties consequently declined. The terms of tenancy as set out in the rent books changes in detail over the years, but one clause persists from 1892 to 1961: 'all rags, hair and other solid matter must be thrown on the ash heap; not into the drains'. The only concession the 1961 book makes is to add 'not put into the WC'! *(John Puttock)*

Left: 62 Sydney Road, 4 October 2003. Two-up two-down with a privy at the end of the garden, they were small but solidly built and comfortable. Today they have been extended at the rear to incorporate bathrooms and a few new houses have been squeezed on to what were fairly long gardens, but little has changed from the front. For almost seventy years 62 Sydney Road was rented by members of the same family. John Redwood (see p. 35) was a police constable who moved to Sutton from Wellington in Somerset. He married Miss Emily Jane Appleton and they had six children, one of whom, Ada, was born in 1884. When Ada Redwood married and became Ada Osman the young couple continued to live with her parents at number 62. Ada in fact lived there for the rest of her life: she died in 1961 and rent ceased to be paid in her name after May of that year. *(George Hobbs)*

2

Steeples & Peoples

Catholic Church of Our Lady of the Rosary, corner of Bramley Road and St Barnabas' Road, 1904. Compare this view with the lower picture on p. 122 to see how much has changed. The presbytery and the houses along Carshalton Road are just visible to the right and left of the photograph respectively. Our Lady of the Rosary was built in 1892 and pre-dates the Catholic Westminster Cathedral by three years; the cathedral's foundation stone was laid on 29 June 1895. Then, as now, the Catholic community in Sutton falls within the Roman Catholic Archdiocese of Southwark served by St George's Cathedral. The Church of Our Lady of the Rosary was the founder church for all the other Catholic churches in the area.

(Author's collection)

The spiritual life of a community is often indicative of its richness and diversity. Sutton has a large number of places of worship serving many faiths and sects. Apart from the Church of England building which gives it its name, St Barnabas' Road alone has buildings dedicated to worshippers in the Church in Wales, the Spiritualist Church and the largest Roman Catholic church in the area. Elsewhere in the town are the Salvation Army citadel and the Religious Society of Friends (Quakers) Meeting House, while the Greek Orthodox community worships in part of the parish church reserved for its use. Sutton's Jewish community has its own synagogue and has been contributing to the life of the town since the Second World War. There is neither Hindu temple, Church of Jesus Christ of the Latter Day Saints (Mormons), nor temple for the Jehovah's Witnesses in Sutton, although they are available nearby. Neither is there a mosque in the town, but the largest mosque in western Europe is just over the border in Morden, so Sutton's Moslem community doesn't have far to go.

Sutton's parish church is St Nicholas', rather overshadowed by the more recent taller buildings surrounding it. There has been a church on the site since Saxon times, although it has been rebuilt several times as the town grew in size and importance. The stoop on the east wall of the lady chapel is very old and was found in the churchyard in the 1920s. It dates from the thirteenth century. Domesday Book says that there were originally two churches belonging to Sutton, one on this site and one probably at Horley which, although 14 miles away, was an outlying estate belonging to and administered by the Manor of Sutton. The current parish church dates from 1864 when the previous building was pulled down and a larger church built to accommodate the growing number of Sutton residents. The building has changed relatively little although the plain glass windows on the north side are a reminder of the bomb that fell in the churchyard on the night of 24 September 1940 and blew out all the windows on that side. The east window was put in when the church was built and is the only original window in the building. It was given by Lady Morrison and she is depicted in it about half-way down on the right in an attitude very similar to that depicted on her memorial to the right of the church's entrance door.

Little of the pre-1864 building remains in the new one, although some of the old monuments and memorials have been transferred from the old church. The old wooden seat within the sanctuary and to the left of the altar is thought to have survived from the previous building's furnishing. In the wood of the old seat is carved: 'Thomas Mynat is my name and with my knife I cut the same. Ann Dom 1655'. I'll bet he got into trouble! Perhaps the sermons of Henry Wyche, rector at the time, were particularly long and boring.

Unusually for a religious foundation of that age, St Nicholas' Church is not built on the top of the hill. That distinction goes to Trinity URC/Methodist church which strangers to the town would be forgiven for mistaking for the parish church. Not only is it in a prominent site but it's also a very imposing building. Designed by Gordon & Gunton, well-known Methodist architects of the time, the church is built of Kentish ragstone and has a crown and lantern spire rather like the sixteenth-century crown on St Giles' cathedral Edinburgh.

Less imposing but to architects no less unique is the final church in the trio of town centre churches, the Baptist church in Cheam Road. The Baptist church opened in September 1934 and is the successor to the one bought by Ernest Shinner on the corner of Hill Road and demolished so that he could extend his store. Before building work began the church meeting resolved 'that the total overall cost of the enterprise should not exceed the amount secured by the sale of the existing site and buildings'. They were successful. When the final costs were reckoned up the church had £30 19s 7d left over.

It is difficult to realise that the design of what appears now as a modest brick and tile building caused a sensation not only locally but in church and architectural circles nationwide. The architect was Nugent Cachemaille-Day whose expressionist modern churches were the most innovative ecclesiastical buildings of the 1930s. Cachemaille-Day was influenced by the Arts and Crafts movement as well as the moderne style popular in Europe in the 1930s. The dark brick exterior is a deliberate contrast with the light spaciousness inside.

The three town-centre churches are not only close together geographically but also spiritually. On 14 January 2001 the Revd Sara Goatcher, Rector of St Nicholas' Church of England, the Revd Martin Camroux, Minister of the Trinity URC/Methodist Church and the Revd Michael Dales, Sutton Baptist Minister formed the Local Ecumenical Partnership (LEP). The ministers officiate in each other's churches and work under the banner of never doing anything separately that they could do together. They even have a monthly magazine called *Unite* – other churches take note!

Fine ecclesiastical architecture is not restricted to the town centre. To the north All Saints, Benhilton, commands the hilltop of Thomas Alcock's new middle-class area (see p. 45), while Christchurch serves the needs of the slightly less prosperous but quickly growing population of south Sutton. In March 1876 a temporary iron church was built on Brighton Road, probably supplied by Humphrey's Iron Churches of London who were specialists in manufacturing temporary religious buildings for growing areas of population. The Revd Herbert Turner became rector of the new church and stayed for ten years before moving to become rector of Sutton's parish church (see p. 32). Two years later, in 1888, the road that became Christchurch Park was laid out on what had been a track through fields, and Christchurch was built.

Designed by Newman Jacques, the red brick building had no tower but did not lack prominence as it was built at the top of a slight rise in the ground. The rectory was built on the southern corner of Christchurch Park and Brighton Road. It, like all the Victorian housing along Christchurch Park, has been demolished and replaced by blocks of flats and modern houses. Even with its narthex, baptistery and porch-cum-tower base, which were added to the west end in about 1910, modern building development means that Christchurch no longer dominates the surrounding area.

St Nicholas' Church, architect's drawing, pre-1864. There has been a church on this site since Saxon times, although the current church dates from 1864. It was designed by Edwin Nash so presumably the drawing is in his hand. Although the building is accurate, the churchyard is not: the Gibson tomb (see back cover) should appear on the left. A curious custom has been connected with the Gibson tomb since 1777 but was discontinued from 2004 for health and safety reasons. Mary Gibson left £500 in consolidated bank stock to Christ's Hospital on the understanding that a representative of the hospital governors opened the tomb on 12 August every year to check that all was in good order. If they fail to do so the legacy passes to the Foundling Hospital. *(Courtesy St Nicholas' Church)*

Raise the Roof appeal, 2003. Congregations today are often distracted from their real work of serving the community by the need to conserve the buildings in their care. After almost 150 years the roof of St Nicholas' was in desperate need of some care and attention. The parochial church council came up with the idea of selling church tiles, the purchaser receiving a Roof Tile Certificate signed by the Rector, the Revd Sara Goatcher. The new 'owner' of the tile then had the opportunity to write something on the reverse of their tile in indelible ink. Each of these inscriptions, dedications or prayers are now contained within the fabric of the building and wait to provide a snapshot of the community, its character and concerns, to historians of the twenty-second century and beyond. *(Courtesy St Nicholas' Church)*

Right: The new roof of St Nicholas' Church, 2003. And this is what it was all about. Efforts have been made to keep the new roof in character with its Victorian predecessor and the patterning is particularly successful. Most people would not agree with the opinion of Nikolaus Pevsner who described the building as 'flint, with broach-spire, not attractive'! *(George Hobbs)*

Below: The Service of Dedication for the new roof on 6 December 2003. The 6th is the feast day of St Nicholas and the Rt Revd Nicholas' Baines officiated on St Nicholas's day in St Nicholas Church – a lovely idea. Left to right are Lesley Pynor, who did much of the organisation, the Revd Sara Goatcher, rector of St Nicholas' Church, Bishop Nick, Bishop of Croydon and the Saint himself. Many people know that St Nicholas developed into 'Santa Claus' and so it comes as no surprise that St Nicholas is the patron saint of children. He is also patron saint of young boys, virgins, pawnbrokers, sailors, prisoners, prostitutes, apothecaries, perfumiers and Russia – more causes than any other saint. *(George Hobbs)*

Dashwood Hall, mid-1960s. The Religious Society of Friends (Quakers) met in this building from 1932 to 1940. Friends came from Purley, Epsom, Mitcham and Muswell Hill to a meeting on 22 November 1932 where one seemed to sum up the ideal: 'If the Quakers have something to give which is vital to the people of Sutton, then they will take root and grow and witness to the power of the living God. But if they are merely going to begin a little Quaker Meeting, another small denomination, then I for one have no time for this concern.' By the time this photograph was taken the building had been taken over by the Sutton and Cheam Division of the Surrey Branch of the Red Cross. *(Courtesy of The Religious Society of Friends)*

Dashwood Hall, Carshalton Road, 21 December 2003. It's ironic that a hall once used by a pacifist society and then by one dedicated to healing, is now a centre for violent sport. The Sutton Martial Arts Centre teaches karate and aikido – a way of using an opponent's energy to defeat them – to both adults and juniors. They also offer yoga, so perhaps the spiritual side is not ignored after all. *(George Hobbs)*

Above: Friends' Meeting House, Worcester Gardens, early 1960s. In February 1940 William 'Tubby' Curtis, alerted the Meeting to a 'detached house of eleven rooms' which could be purchased and altered for use as a Meeting House. As treasurer of the Meeting he was also chiefly responsible for raising the necessary funds. The first meeting was held in the new Meeting House on 10 November the same year. Fast work! On their arrival a letter of welcome from the Jewish Synagogue next door said: 'May I express our delight that your Body has once more joined residence with us. May we respectfully accord you a very hearty welcome to "Cedar Road" as you most kindly extended to us in the Worcester Gardens days. And as our aims in many ways seem to run on harmonious lines may "God" grant us the understanding to so carry on in the future.' Amen. *(Courtesy of The Religious Society of Friends)*

Below: Car park, Brighton Road, 21 December 2003. The Friends moved out of their meeting house in 1970 and the building was demolished to be replaced by a car park. IPC Media, which used to inhabit nearby Quadrant House, arranged for its staff to have exclusive use of certain floors to ensure adequate parking. Such an arrangement is no longer in place not least because Reed Business Information, a successor to IPC in Quadrant House, prefers to encourage staff to use public transport. The car park is owned by Sutton Borough Council and has space for 640 cars. *(George Hobbs)*

Meeting for worship, Worcester Gardens, early 1960s. Meeting for worship is central to Quakerism. Outward religious symbols are considered unimportant and a written creed unhelpful; there is no pre-arranged order of service and no paid clergy. Much of the Meeting takes place in silence, although anyone moved to speak is encouraged to do so. The emphasis is always on simplicity and seeking to discover God's will rather than trying to fix it in words. Friends meeting included: 1, Arthur White; 2, Jenny Steel; 3, May Lambert; 4, Alys Peterson; 5, Isabel Boag; 6, Mollie Abbott; 7, Jack Boag; 8, Raymond Forsyth; 9, Olwen Forsyth; 10, Violet Reed; 11, Vivian Vokes; 12, Phyllis Baillie; 13, Margaret Vokes; 14, Martin Wilson; 15, Peter Barns; 16, Arthur Ware; 17, Ann Barns; 18, Donald Doerr; 19, Frances Hill; 20, Edna White; 21, Fred Hanant; 22, Ronald Abbott; 23, Cecil Heath. *(Courtesy of The Religious Society of Friends)*

Outside broadcast unit, Cedar Road, January 1980. A live meeting for worship was broadcast from Sutton meeting house as the morning service on Radio 4. Introducing the meeting an announcer explained, 'You cannot broadcast silence.' (One wonders why not. Perhaps the producer was concerned that anyone tuning in late would assume a fault in the transmission.) A controller sitting in the room played pre-recorded music audible to listeners but not heard by the worshippers. Four microphones were placed in the centre of the room and those who spoke had to come forward and pause while the music was silenced. There were around six spoken contributions in the forty-minute service. *(Courtesy of The Religious Society of Friends)*

Friends' Meeting House, Cedar Road, 31 March 2004. The Friends moved here from Worcester Gardens on 1 April 1970. As well as being the base for the Sutton Quaker Meeting, the Meeting House is used by a wide range of non-Quaker organisations, including a healing group, Alcoholics Anonymous, the Women's Institute, the Humanists, Sutton Peace and Justice Group and many others. Central to the Quaker faith is the belief that all people are equal and equally worthy of respect and this is demonstrated by the disparate number of organisations which use their premises. *(George Hobbs)*

Left: Sutton's new synagogue, Cedar Road, 1964. Sutton has been home to a Jewish community since the 1930s when people began holding services in each other's homes. One of the first meeting places was, a small hut at the back of Sutton railway station. The community's first synagogue was consecrated in October 1945 at Wellesley Lodge, 62 Brighton Road. Mr Harold Perloff remembers: 'In the mid '40s my father bought a rambling, dilapidated old building with the intention that we would move into it. The local Jewish community approached my father to ask if there was some space available to turn into a *shul* [synagogue]. Our family moved into a small cottage in the grounds and the big house was made available to house the *shul.*' From Wellesley Lodge the community moved to Worcester Gardens and, when the council proposed to build a car park on the site, moved again to Cedar Road. (*June Lewis, Synagogue archives*)

Induction of Rabbi Avrohom Groner, 29 June 2003. The Chief Rabbi, Dr Jonathan Sacks, addresses the Sutton community from the pulpit of the *shul* in Cedar Road. Rabbi Groner, pictured right with his wife Shternie, was 29 when he was inducted to the Sutton Synagogue pulpit and the Chief Rabbi congratulated Sutton on the appointment of such an enthusiastic and vibrant young rabbi. Around 300 people were invited to participate in this special event including Sutton dignitaries, VIPs and rabbis from as far away as South Africa and Israel. (*June Lewis, Synagogue archives*)

Sutton cheder, early 1950s. A cheder is a room or school where Hebrew is taught. Jews have always placed great emphasis on education and the study of God's laws and every *shul* has its own cheder to teach children from the local community. This picture shows the Sutton cheder when the *shul* was still in Worcester Gardens. Students included in the photograph are Helen Woolfe, Francis Austin, Naomi Frickers, Andrew Perloff, Norman Shaw, Michael Prizant, Harold Perloff, Rosalyn Frickers, Natalie Kleinman and Barbara Goldstein. *(June Lewis, Synagogue archives)*

Teachers of Sutton cheder, 1957. Pictured are Ruth Koschland, Dayan Steinberg, Rev Maurice Rose (later to gain qualifications to become Rabbi Rose) and Jill Ison. Rev Rose was noted for visiting members of the community on his motorbike as he had no car at the time. Today the Sutton cheder is divided into four classes and has about twenty-four children aged 5 to 12. The standard of Hebrew education in Sutton is very high and children invariably win awards and prizes presented by the United Synagogue Education Board. *(June Lewis, Synagogue archives)*

Ladies Guild outing, early 1950s. An official Ladies Guild was formed in 1946 under the chairmanship of Eileen Fishman who held the post for ten years until she was succeeded by Fay Silver. By 1955 the guild had eighty-five members, which must have been virtually every wife in the community at the time. Pictured are Claire Landau, Sarah Levitt, Fay Perloff, Hannah Davis, Naomi Grunwald, Lily Reef, Lily Novitt, Eve Simmonds, Debbie Goldstein, Miki Selby, Eileen Fishman, Annie Ozin, Millicent Taffel, Mrs Nathan, Ray Bennett, Ray Dias, Ida Shaw, Celia Korklin, Rae Prizant, Betty Levy, Betty Beaver, Hazel Symons, Anne Cohen and Betty Perl. On the twenty-fifth anniversary of the opening of the synagogue Mrs Fishman remembered: 'After the end of the Second World War there was a wave of enthusiasm from the local Jewish Community . . . to create a synagogue and forum where Jews of every age could participate. The Ladies Guild ran regular functions to raise the necessary money.' There is now a growing membership of the League of Jewish Women, an organisation outside the synagogue, members of which do a variety of welfare work within and outside the community and also raise money for local charities, Jewish and non-Jewish alike. The community has come a long way from the time when a 1944 invitation to a Purim celebration concluded with the plea, 'Please bring some cakes'! *(June Lewis, Synagogue archives)*

Above: The Catholic Church of Our Lady of the Rosary, 1904. The church (left) with its presbytery (right) was the first built to serve the Catholic community in Sutton. As the area became more densely populated the large parish was divided into smaller parishes each with a Catholic church of its own. Newtown was laid out by Lord of the Manor, Thomas Alcock, as working-class housing. It was his lack of real interest and control over development in the area which led eventually to permission being granted for the establishment of a Catholic church at a time when the faith was still viewed with some suspicion. Worship began on the site in 1882 in a temporary church possibly dedicated to St Mary. The current church was built a decade later. *(Courtesy of the Church of Our Lady of the Rosary)*

Below: The Catholic Church of Our Lady of the Rosary, 21 December 2003. The church and presbytery are recognisably the same although the parish centre, built in 1995, now fills what was once the garden as well as taking over much of the ground floor of the presbytery. It's good to see that the pillar box still does sentry duty on the corner and that at least two of the roadside trees still exist. *(George Hobbs)*

The Catholic Church of Our Lady of the Rosary, interior, 1904. As originally built the church was some 50ft shorter than it is now and lacked a north aisle. During the early part of its life the building doubled as a school during the week and a church on Sunday. Two Catholic schools were built in the area at about this time: St Mary's Primary School in Shorts Road and St Philomena's High School for Girls founded by the Daughters of the Cross in Carshalton House. Pupils from the school housed in Our Lady of the Rosary probably went to either depending on age. *(Courtesy of the Church of Our Lady of the Rosary)*

The Catholic Church of Our Lady of the Rosary, interior, 13 December 2003. Nikolaus Pevsner says that E. Ingress Bell extended the chancel in 1887 but this is inaccurate as the permanent church was not built until five years later. The architect, at least for the additions to the chancel, was John Hawes who later entered a Catholic monastic order. Plans for the hexagonal extension were drawn up in August 1912 and built shortly afterward. It formed a higher chancel at the east end of the church allowing the altar to be raised and the whole area to be lightened. *(George Hobbs)*

Reredos, high altar, Catholic Church of Our Lady of the Rosary, 13 December 2003. The reredos reaches nearly as high as the 40ft ceiling and is very impressive. It is made out of Carrara marble inlaid with mosaic tessera. Marble is a loose term given to calcite or dolomite crystals produced by subjecting limestone to heat and pressure. Prized since the early Roman period, Carrara marble is valued by sculptors for its whiteness and consistent purity; Michelangelo's 'David' is sculpted from it. More than 300 marble quarries are still located in the Carrara mountains, which produce more than 500,000 tonnes of marble per year. Leonardo da Vinci invented the marble cutting machine which, with the addition of electricity, is still used today. *(George Hobbs)*

Reredos, lady chapel, Catholic Church of Our Lady of the Rosary, 13 December 2003. Each altar in the church is backed by a mosaic reredos. This page pictures those from the high altar and the Lady Chapel and there is also one in the north aisle in the Chapel of the Sacred Heart. Black and white photography cannot do justice to the magnificence of the colour and detail. Here the Virgin Mary, cloaked in blue and surrounded by rainbow colours picked out in gold, is assumed into heaven. *(George Hobbs)*

3

The Best Days
of Your Life?

Winners of a schools competition, 20 June 1987. The Sutton District Water Company organised a competition for schools that visited them during water week. The water company still organises visits to its treatment works and has a team of trained tutors who visit schools and give talks and demonstrations by request. Pictured left to right are Keith Simmonds, Director and General Manager of Sutton District Water Company, John Cullen, Sadaf Khan, Sharon Smith, Laura Wells, Colin Lee, Elizabeth Fleet, Tracy Banks, Richard Pearson, Zoe Sparks, Michele Galland and Waiphyo Kyaw. *(Courtesy of Sutton and East Surrey Water)*

Sutton is noted for its education. As early as 1841 when Sutton was still a small agricultural town, owing much of its existence to meeting the needs of passengers on the turnpike road, it nevertheless had 170 children attending the parish schools. As today, the local residents of a century ago had a wide choice of schools to which to send their children. The parish schools and board schools catered for those who lacked the money to pay for their children's education, while at the other end of the social scale were private schools and seminaries for those who could afford them.

One 'high class ladies school for resident and non-resident pupils' was Eversfield. It was run by Mrs E.L. Mortimer and originally situated halfway between Sherwood Park Road and Robin Hood Lane. In 1933 the school moved to 45 Mulgrave Road and took over premises that had been a private hotel called Raven's Court. Eversfield School closed during the Second World War, but in 1946 Eversfield House reopened as a residential home for the elderly. It is now run by the Sutton and Cheam Elderly People's Housing Association, a charitable trust providing 'accommodation for elderly persons of limited means'.

At one time many schools were owned and run by their principal who set the syllabus according to what they thought important for children to learn. Eversfield, for example, prepared girls for matriculation or university entrance examinations, but also stressed health, manners and habits of neatness. (Modern schools take note!) Benhilton College and Kindergarten at 1 and 2 Burnell Road didn't aim so high and taught its pupils English Language and Literature, French, German, drawing and singing. At the end of the nineteenth century Sutton had a large number of privately owned educational establishments. These included a boarding and day school run by Miss J. Fraser at 2 Carshalton Villas, Carshalton Road; Beaufort House School also in Carshalton Road about 20 yards from the corner of Lind Road, run by the Misses Ellingham; and the Sutton Conservatoire of Music & Art run by Madame Costa on the corner of Cheam Road and Robin Hood Lane. Madame Costa may even have employed Miss S.A. Martin, 'professor of violin and piano', who lived across town at 4 Lewis Villas.

Child protection laws and the dictates of the national curriculum have meant that privately owned schools are much more of a rarity. Stowford College on Brighton Road is housed in one of the very earliest buildings erected south of the railway line and is an exception. At one time the glebe of the rectory of Christchurch lay to the north and a similarly imposing house called Beechurst stood in wooded grounds to the south. Both have now gone – Devonshire Avenue runs roughly east to west through Beechurst – and only Stowford remains. The college has around 100 pupils aged between 6 and 16 and offers a particularly well-structured dyslexic programme. Most of the schools in Sutton have pupils from a range of ethnic backgrounds and Stowford College is no exception. The Independent Schools Inspectorate report from November 2003, which is an independent school's equivalent of Ofsted, notes approvingly that 'in the junior department pupils are greeted at registration in German, French, Afrikaans and Japanese and reply in the same languages'.

The first nursery school in the world was opened by Robert Owen in New Lanark in 1816. Even though Owen was Welsh, Wales had to wait until the 1930s – another 120 years – before the first Welsh nursery school was opened by the charity

Save the Children. Sutton had one of the earliest nursery schools in England, funded by the great educational philanthropist Thomas Wall, he of sausages and ice cream. The exact date of the opening of the nursery school seems debatable: historians put it at 1909, while the school's Ofsted report states that it was established in 1914. The earlier date seems more likely; would anyone have been founding nursery schools when the country was about to go to war? Perhaps they would as it may have acted rather as a crèche would today, for young working women whose men were away.

For many years the Thomas Wall Nursery School was situated very near West Street, at the west end of George Street. The school still exists, although it now shares accommodation with Robin Hood Infants' School. The original building was demolished towards the end of the 1990s and sheltered accommodation built on the vacant plot. Use of the site may have changed but the name is not forgotten; the new cul de sac is named Thomas Wall Close. As at Eversfield, the young have given way to the elderly but it doesn't mean that activities are any less fun. On 11 June 2004 residents at Thomas Wall Close were joined by Sutton's mayor, Councillor Tony Brett Young, to take part in a national attempt to set a new world record for the largest simultaneous tea party. I wonder who did the washing up.

Thomas Wall was committed to what today would be called lifelong learning and, as well as founding the nursery school which bears his name, made major contributions to the Adult School Movement. The first adult school is said to have been opened in Nottingham in 1798 to teach young women working in the lace and hosiery factories. Sutton's Adult School opened in 1895 in what is now Benhill Avenue and was one of about 350 such schools in the country offering classes in the evenings and on Sundays to working men and women. Adult Schools were the first organisations to offer education designed specifically for adults and involving discussion, encouragement and debate. The people of Sutton must have been eager to take advantage of such provision as only four years later the Technical Institute was opened in Throwley Road (see p. 70)

Adult education is still encouraged in Sutton, which has one of the very few purpose-built centres for adult learning in the country. Sutton College of Liberal Arts (SCOLA) was formed in 1972 when all the adult education in the borough was united in one organisation. Locals who do not want to take part in structured learning also benefit; the college library doubles as the public library and is reputed to be the largest of its kind in the country. In 2001 the college changed its name to Sutton College of Learning for Adults and in 2003 over 12,000 people registered for one or more of the 1,000 courses on offer. SCOLA continues the tradition started by the Adult School Movement of offering the opportunity and satisfaction of continuing education to adults in the local community.

Above: The official opening of Sutton County School and Technical Institute, Throwley Road, 21 July 1899. The building was state-of-the-art for the time and designed to hold 150 boys during the day and 300 adult students in the evening. (One wonders why adult students appeared to need less room!) Lord Middleton, the Lord Lieutenant of Surrey, who formally opened the building, declared that there had been nothing comparable at Eton when he was one of its pupils. Harold Elgar, the 13-year-old son of the local postmaster, registered as its first pupil on 12 September 1899. The building was demolished when Throwley Way was built in the 1980s and the site is now the back of Wilkinson (see p. 30). *(Courtesy Sutton Grammar School)*

Below: Sutton County School, Manor Lane, *c.* 1928. The school had been subjected to severe overcrowding at its Throwley Road site for some time, prompting the Headmaster Mr Cockshutt to expostulate: 'I believe that the protest against the present very inadequate buildings is annual.' One of his pupils, Roger C. Baker, commented, 'We had seen the new school going up on the allotments below the school field and very soon we were carrying science and other equipment down Throwley Road and into this pristine building. What passers-by thought to see crocodiles of school boys carrying retort stands, boxes of test tubes and other impedimenta!' *(Courtesy Sutton Grammar School)*

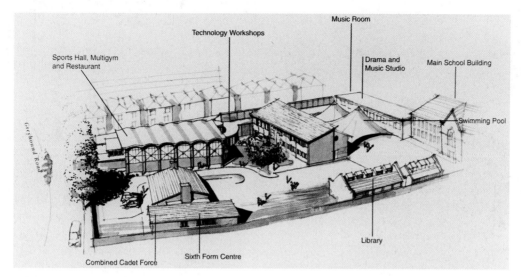

Above: Architect's drawings of the proposed expansion to Sutton Grammar School, 1993. The playing field has been superseded by much larger and more suitable premises in Northey Avenue. The area is now a hard surface and offers the school the opportunity for its first major expansion since the premises were originally built. (*Courtesy Latham Architects and Sutton Grammar School*)

Right: Humanities block, 31 March 2004. The humanities block is visible in the centre of the architects' plans above. It and the technology workshops were completed in 1997. They are situated just about where the groundsman is working in the photograph opposite. (*George Hobbs*)

Right: Sutton County School swimming team, 1914. In 1903 the Sutton Swimming Baths was built next to the school and the boys were eager to take advantage of the facilities. In 1914 they won the Surrey Secondary Schools Senior Challenge Cup, but this proved a mere foretaste of what was to come. The following year Sutton County School became the first school to win all four trophies in the Inter-Schools' Competition. Back row, left to right: Mr Hensley (headmaster), Mr Howard, Mr Martin. Middle row: C. Barni, S.N. Levitt (see p. 73), H.W. Lloyd, E.G. Savage. Front row: C. Narbeth, P.L. Cooper. The Savages were a family of brothers all of whom swam well: L. Savage, also a pupil at the school, was the national schoolboy freestyle champion in 1913. (*Courtesy Sutton Grammar School*)

School caps, 6 December 2003. These four caps were all worn by boys at the school. From the top down are the caps of -?-, H. Meredith, J.A. Connolly, R Wadmore. The unnamed cap probably dates from around 1900 as pictures of boys wearing similar caps appear in the earliest school photographs from that date. Meredith's cap is the only one which is dated – he wore it from 1912 to 14 – and another school photograph shows a Meredith, initial unspecified, as a prefect in 1914. Unfortunately this Meredith is not wearing a cap, but the tassel is an addition so perhaps it indicates prefect status. Jack Connolly and his brothers Mike and Tim became members of Cheam Cricket Club and are pictured at a Cricket Club dinner in 1956. Wadmore's cap no longer carries the SCS monogram of Sutton County School, but the Athene Owl of the Grammar School as it was now permitted to be called. Wadmore too was a prefect and, as the stripe beneath the badge indicates, in Brown House. Caps ceased to be worn by anyone beyond the third form in 1961 and the practice was discontinued entirely shortly afterwards. *(George Hobbs)*

Athene Owl, school crest, 21 December 2003. The owl pictured is the Little Owl (*Athene noctua*), successfully reintroduced to Northamptonshire from the Netherlands in 1889, with further introductions into Yorkshire, Hampshire and Hertfordshire at the turn of the century. They are the smallest of the resident owls and are just a little larger than a blackbird. In Greek mythology the Little Owl was the messenger of Athene, the goddess of wisdom, and they are still reputed to nest in cavities in the wall of the Acropolis, Athene's temple. No one seems to know why the owl was chosen as the school badge – perhaps its introduction to Britain at about the time the school was founded caught the early school's imagination – but the motto 'Keep Faith' was added in 1954. This view of the emblem appears on the school gates, which were donated by Old Suttonians to commemorate the school's centenary in 1999. *(George Hobbs)*

Cadet Corps, *c.* 1940. The school Cadet Corps was created in February 1915 and, with the occasional interruption, military training in one form or another has flourished ever since. The July 1916 copy of the school magazine published two poems by Sydney Neville Levitt, known as 'Doddler' (see swimming group, p. 71). A couple of lines from his 'Decorum Est' sum up the attitude of the time: 'Athene whom we loved has gone away / And Mars has come to be our leader now.' Levitt, a good all-rounder at school, joined the Royal Fusiliers in 1916 and rose to the rank of subaltern. He was killed on 29 September 1918. He was 19.

In this view the gentleman with the walking stick is R.A. Lloyd, German master and organiser of extra-curricular boxing, who eventually served the school for more than thirty years. From 1928 to 1939 Mr Lloyd together with Mr F.G. Wells arranged tours abroad most frequently to Switzerland. Mr Lloyd recalled: 'We walked fifteen to twenty miles a day with full pack and spent each night in a different youth hostel. As a rule we arranged two rest days in the fortnight at some place of special interest.' Pictured with him are W.H. Battons, H.A. Davies, J.M. Ewen, J. Goff, P.W. Harris, D. Hocking, J.D. Honer, A. Lands, R.G. Ledger, L.D. Loan, J.S. Malpas, P.T.S. Matthews, V. Matthews, J.C. Moss, P.H. Newman, R.A. Pomroy, C.V. Pomroy, W.G. Sawyer, D.A. Shaw, G.R. Smyth, K.J. Snow, M. Sutcliffe, D.E. Waple and possibly P.W. Cox, W. Donbar and ? Gardner. *(Courtesy Sutton Grammar School)*

Amateur dramatics, Sutton Grammar School, 1923. The school's Amateur Dramatic and Operatic Society was formed in 1924, but the tradition of providing light entertainment had started much earlier. The plot of *St Patrick's Day* has disappeared into the mists of time but lacked too many female characters to confound an all-boys school! Left to right, back row: T.A.M. Pink, A. Good, R. Warren, R.W. Goff, C.H. Fenn, F. Robson, H.A. Syndercombe, W.G. Seal. Front row: J.E. Lee, W.F. Waters, A.D. Coombs, G.L. Richmond, A. Graham. Reginald Goff went on to become a noted high court judge, while at the time of writing Mr Syndercombe is still alive and now in his nineties. *(Courtesy Sutton Grammar School)*

Amateur dramatics, Sutton High School, 3 April 1894. The play in question is *The Heir at Law* or *£20,000 in the lottery* written by George Colman the Younger. Colman was a successful playwright and theatre manager and later became censor of plays for the Lord Chamberlain. Standing, left to right: Helen Page, Alice Collins, Katie Orwen (playing Zekiel Homespun), Ethel Atkins, Miss Bell. Seated, left to right: Frances West, Hettie Mackereth, Edith Overton, Sybil Atkins, Rose Sprules. *(Courtesy Sutton High School)*

Little Shop of Horrors, joint production by Sutton High School and Sutton Grammar School, 2000. In 1949 Sutton Grammar School for Boys first combined with Sutton High School for Girls to produce *The Pirates of Penzance* and joint musicals are now presented biennially. *Little Shop of Horrors* is written by Howard Ashman with music by Alan Menken. It tells the story of orphan skid-row florist Seymour Krelbourn who discovers an exotic plant with a very unusual appetite. Screamingly funny, the musical comedy was like a cross between *The Day of the Triffids* and *Kiss me Kate*. (*Courtesy Sutton High School*)

Sutton High School, *c.* 1900. The building on the right was Park House, originally owned by Edward Solly and leased to the Girls' Public Day School Company in 1883. On 17 January 1884, with Miss Whyte heading a staff of eight teachers, the school opened to eighty girls. Next door to Park House but not in the photograph stood a pair of houses very similar to each other called Suffolk House and Norfolk House. Suffolk House was purchased by Sutton High School in 1932 to house the juniors; Norfolk House became a hotel until it was demolished in 1963. The two houses had bay windows architecturally very similar to those in the centre of the photograph, which has caused some confusion over identification. However, they also both had circular drives which make them easily identifiable on maps of the time. *(Courtesy Sutton High School)*

Sutton High School, 31 March 2004. Details have changed of course and the school has grown, but the buildings are still recognisable. The main change is the removal of the top storey of the building in the middle of the picture as it had become dangerous (see p. 78). Today Sutton High School is small enough to tailor teaching to the individual needs of its pupils, and large enough to offer a wide curriculum taught by specialist teachers. It is one of twenty-five independent girls' schools in the Girls' Day School Trust. *(George Hobbs)*

Teaching staff, Sutton High School, *c.* 1910. The staff are pictured in front of a pavilion which once stood in the gardens of the school when its buildings were less extensive and Sutton itself far more rural. Back row, left to right: M. Curtis, D. Bott, D. Compton, B.C. Fry, K. Hancock, E.M. Thomas, E. Magratti, E. Elliot. Middle row: P.J.M. Taytor, A.B. Hunt (see p. 78), C.M.R. Callender, V. Henry (headmistress), I. Berst, J. Bruce-Veker, M.E. Browne. Front row, left to right: G.E. Wright, M.E. Smith, M.C. Hill, E.M.L. Leed, I. Gillespie, F.R. Eaman. Only Miss Callender looks as though she's enjoying the experience! *(Courtesy Sutton High School)*

'Rough Daddy', Christmas 2003. Stephen Callaghan has only been the headmaster of Sutton High since September 2003 and is the first male head in the school's history. He already seems to have made quite an impression! Teaching staff are much more relaxed about their image than they were a century ago but rap is still restricted to the end-of-term entertainment. Mr Callaghan was apparently very good but the school might have to wait some time before he appears on TOTP. *(Courtesy Sutton High School)*

Science lesson, Sutton High School, *c.* 1900. Far right is Miss A.D. Hunt (see p. 77) who was the school's senior science mistress from September 1895 to July 1928. This room became the school library in the autumn of 1925 when a new laboratory was opened, which is itself now the dining room. The windows to the left are the dormer windows in the central block of the school pictured on p. 76. The room no longer exists as it was in the part of the building removed for safety reasons. Note the very early models of atoms (nucleus orbited by particle), or possibly simple orreries, hanging from the ceiling. The girls were taught thrift as well as science, as Liptons Tea and Golden Syrup tins are being used for heating substances on the Bunsen burners. *(Courtesy Sutton High School)*

Art lesson, Sutton High School, *c.* 1900. This, the old studio, was used from 1885 to 1935 when a new one was built. The girls are probably drawing the flowers in the vase on the small table; figure drawing from life was not considered acceptable for girls so they are unlikely to be drawing their teacher. Around the wall are plaster casts of classical figures, animals and plants to provide a variety of 3D models for the pupils to copy. Note the relatively large number of gas mantles; the room would need to be brightly lit if used for artwork. *(Courtesy Sutton High School)*

Cricket team, Sutton High School, 1934. Back row, left to right: Ruth Berlandina, Mary Bennet, Frances Head, Mary Beaumont, Una Park. Middle row: Sheila Young, Brenda Canning, ? Walkiden, Nancy Glover, Rose Ruberry. Front row: Doris Isaby, Monica Eldridge. Judging by the pads she's wearing, Mary Beaumont was the wicket keeper. Misses Berlandina, Park, Young and Eldridge all went to Dartford College of Physical Education just as that college's students were permitted to work for the University of London's Diploma in Theory and Practice of Physical Education. Founded in 1885 in Hampstead and transferring to Dartford a decade later, the college was the brainchild of Martina Bergman Österberg who was passionate about female emancipation. Interestingly the gym tunics as worn by the girls in this photograph were 'invented' by Martina Österberg in 1892. Those of Sutton High School were navy with a purple sash. *(Courtesy Sutton High School)*

Year 8 Design and Technology (D&T) class, 2003. Helen Thorpe uses a pillar drill to bore holes in a wooden plank. Safety is very important when using heavy-duty machinery; all D&T students must wear goggles, and fingers are protected from the drill by a guard. Sutton High School does well in school league tables, but its pupils are successful in extra-curricular activities too. Felicity Yeoh, year 13, was the youngest of five winners in the BBC competition to write a story based on Chaucer's *Canterbury Tales*. Her story 'The Oldest Tale' was inspired by 'The Wife of Bath's Tale' and was broadcast on Radio 4 on 4 February 2004. *(Courtesy Sutton High School)*

The Robin Hood Junior School team that won the Sutton Borough Road Safety competition, 1969. The school took over buildings formerly used by Sutton West High School and was officially opened on 9 July 1969. In its first year Robin Hood Junior won the borough seven-a-side football, took part in fundraising for Help the Aged and visited Le Touquet as well as winning the road safety quiz. The picture shows A and B teams and reserves. (*Courtesy Robin Hood Junior School*)

Environmental project, 2001. Begun in 2001, the project was the brainchild of Jackie Browne, senior midday supervisor and classroom assistant at Robin Hood Junior. The trees were donated by Shirley Faulkner and helping to plant them are, left to right: Daniel Temple, Louise Bryant-Cue and Andre Fernandez. With the help of Sutton Ecology Centre, pupils from the school use their lunch hours to grow vegetables and fruit and have developed a wild flower area including a pond. The project will provide future children with the opportunity to learn about the importance of caring for the environment. (*Courtesy Robin Hood Junior School*)

Robin Hood Junior School, *c.* 1970. Skipping? Or a sports day finishing tape? The children seem to be enjoying the activity whatever it is. Much of the architecture of the school remains the same today, although an increase in the number of pupils has meant that mobile classrooms have had to be installed on part of the ground. The archway in the background no longer exists as it and the part of the field where the photographer is standing is now under St Nicholas Way (see p. 31). *(Courtesy Robin Hood Junior School)*

Above: Robin Hood Junior School visit to Hindleap Warren, 12 May 1994. Hindleap Warren is an outdoor education centre providing a change of scene in which young people can gain experience, instruction and fun. The obstacle course, pictured here, tests teamwork as well as coordination, and it's not far to the ground. *(Courtesy Robin Hood Junior School)*

Right: Robin Hood Junior School visit to Hindleap Warren, 1993. So this is what the staff get up to! Mrs Tighe certainly got more than she bargained for. *(Courtesy Robin Hood Junior School)*

All Saints' Benhilton Church of England Primary School, Benhilton Gardens, looking south, 8 June 1985. This is the old school, which was built as a temporary measure after the previous school buildings were bombed. The school log book for Monday 2 December 1940 says: 'School was closed as the building was damaged by bombs which fell on Friday evening at approximately 10 pm.' Lessons took place in All Saints' Church, from whose tower this view is taken, until alternative arrangements could be made. All Saints' Primary School shared premises with other local schools for almost ten years. This building was dedicated on 20 April 1950 by the Lord Bishop of Southwark and officially opened on 24 May the same year. *(Courtesy All Saints' Benhilton Primary School)*

All Saints' Benhilton Church of England Primary School, All Saints Road, looking east, 8 June 1985. The temporary school was intended to last ten years but survived more than three decades before the present building was constructed. The new school was built on two acres of land next to All Saints' vicarage and was officially opened on 17 March 1986 by the Rt Revd Wilfred Woods, Bishop of Croydon; the bishop retired in 2003. Once the new buildings were in use the old school was demolished and flats built on the site. *(Courtesy All Saints' Benhilton Primary School)*

All Saints' Benhilton Church of England Primary School, Benhilton Gardens, *c.* 1983, founded early in 1866. The headteacher wrote in that year's school log book for 16 February: 'The classification [i.e. placing the children in classes] of the School being now complete I took the opportunity this day of examining the several classes with the view to determining the attainment of each. The result was altogether un-satisfactor.'! *(Courtesy All Saints' Benhilton Primary School)*

Laying the foundation stone for the new school, 21 June 1984. The Rt Revd Keith Sutton (appropriate!), Bishop of Kingston, makes an enthusiastic bricklayer, but he was not the school's first choice. The previous year Simon Parker, a pupil at the school, had written to the Very Revd Robert Runcie, Archbishop of Canterbury, inviting him to wield the trowel. The archbishop replied saying: 'I am sorry that I am unable to come and lay the foundation stone at your school. There are a lot of schools in the Canterbury Diocese to whom I must go from time to time' and went on to add his good wishes for the rebuilding. *(Courtesy All Saints' Benhilton Primary School)*

Left: Morris dancing, 9 June 1982. Mrs Shirley Godson, headteacher at the time, taught morris dancing to many of the children at All Saints' School. Clad in the traditional costume with bells below the knee the boys are demonstrating their prowess at a stick dance. Morris dancing is thought to be a relic of pre-Christian fertility rites; the clashing of the sticks, for example, is intended to scare away malevolent influences. Whatever the origin the pupils are obviously enjoying themselves – look at the concentration on the faces. *(Courtesy All Saints' Benhilton Primary School)*

Below: Cookery class, September 1994. The classes at All Saints' Primary School are all named after trees. Here Chestnut class have collected windfall apples from the field and picked blackberries from the hedgerows. Under the supervision of Miss Witchell they're cooking their own blackberry and apple crumble. The school constantly seeks ways to broaden the pupils' experience and extra-curricular activities have included watching the bathing of a baby, feeding new born lambs and exploring the intricacies of a fire engine. It is a far cry from when the Diocesan Organising Master visited the school on 24 November 1892 and remarked about the lack of good modern desks. *(Courtesy All Saints' Benhilton Primary School)*

Overton Grange School under construction, early summer 1996. The school was constructed on derelict ground that had once held a blood transfusion centre and was then a youth theatre workshop. Contrary to the opinion of some local residents the school encroached very little on the east end of Overton Park, the playing field of the former Greater London Council Staff Association. The photograph shows the steelwork erected for the assembly hall, with the sports hall to the right. Rooms for dance (ground floor) and drama (first floor) are to be built at the side of the assembly hall nearest the camera. *(Courtesy Overton Grange School)*

Overton Grange School, 2 April 2004. There have been three stages of building at Overton Grange. Although the school had its first intake in 1997, it was officially opened by Lord Dearing on 27 March 1998. The second stage of building added the additional accommodation needed for GCSE students plus additional playgrounds. It was completed in September 2000. A third phase of building work added a sixth form which was first opened in September 2002 and the school now has 220 sixth form students. *(George Hobbs)*

Overton Grange School, classroom, *c.* 1997. Much has changed in education over the years. Desks have been replaced by lockers, banks of electric sockets range the walls and whiteboards have replaced blackboards. Good teaching remains central to any school's success however. Here Bridget Elton takes a class in Electronics. (*Courtesy Overton Grange School*)

Opposite, above: First day at Overton Grange School, 4 September 1997. 180 pupils started at the new school, although 210 pupils are now admitted to year 7. Kieran Osborne has been the headteacher since the school's beginning and has seen it grow from these 180 11 year-old students to 1,300 11–19 year olds. For the protection of children government regulations restrict identifying them in photographs, but the staff can be named. Left to right: Sarah Harris, Bridget Elton, Karen Williams (now Kennedy), Alan Barrett, Jo Liddle, Ken Perry, Karl Nicholas, Frances Chave, Peter Wright, Phil Brattle (caretaker), Mark Nearey, Kieran Osborne (headteacher), Chris Pagdin, Rosemary Kington, Janice Harvey, Dawn Connelly (lunchtime supervisor), Clare Heron, unnamed pupil, Rita Money, Jackie South, Catherine Hedger, David Eccles, Cheryl Taylor, unnamed pupil, Brenda Morley (chair of governors). (*Courtesy Overton Grange School*)

Opposite, below: The same students at the end of Key Stage 4, July 2002. The progression of a pupil through school is now plotted by what are called Key Stages. Key Stage 3 consists of the first three years in secondary school where pupils are aged 11–13; Key Stage 4 is the two years which normally make up the GCSE course when pupils are 14–16. Key Stage 5 is the sixth form, i.e. students who are 16–19. Some of the staff who started with the school still remain. Standing at the back, left to right: Mark Walker, Ken Penny, Susan Bostridge, Karen Kennedy (*née* Williams), David Eccles, Bridget Elton, Cheryl Taylor. (*Courtesy Overton Grange School*)

Opposite: Official opening of Robin Hood Infants' School, 9 July 1969. The school had been occupied since September 1968 but was opened officially by Mrs Richard Sharples accompanied by her husband. Here Sir Richard and the school's first headmistress, Isabel Greene, listen to two 6-year-old pupils read. Sir Richard Sharples was appointed governor of Bermuda in October 1972. On 10 March the following year he and his aide-de-camp, Captain Hugh Sayers, were assassinated as they strolled in the grounds of Government House. It was a long way from the safety of Sutton's new infant school. *(Courtesy Robin Hood Infants' School)*

Below: Overton Grange School, staff and governors, 2003. From a teaching complement of twelve in 1997, the staff numbers have increased to around 100 as the school has expanded. It would take far too long to name everyone but the Senior Leadership Team is sitting at the front. From left to right, beginning seventh left, are Keith Stride, Head of Sixth Form; Gerry Bennett, Deputy Head; Brenda Morley, Chair of Governors; Kieran Osborne, Headteacher; Frances Chave, Deputy Head; Ann Dent, Bursar; David Eccles, Head of Guidance and Inclusion. *(Courtesy Overton Grange School)*

West Street School, *c.* 1968. The plaque above the central porch says 'National School 1854'. National Schools were founded in 1811 by Andrew Bell, an Anglican clergyman, and West Street School was certainly supported financially and in religious instruction by St Nicholas' Church. The school originally consisted of a large room on either side of the headteacher's house, one each for the older boys and girls, with a smaller room for infants at the back. In 1879 additional wings were added to each side of West Street School and by 1896 there was room for 118 boys, 118 girls and 100 infants. The school closed in 1968 and was demolished in 1971. *(John Puttock)*

St Nicholas Centre, 7 March 2004. The St Nicholas shopping centre was built over part of West Street so it's difficult to know exactly where the site of West Street School now is, although comparison of old maps show that it must be close to here. This picture shows the south end of the ground floor of the shopping centre. *(George Hobbs)*

4

Tracks, Trolleys & Tyres

The Cock Hotel, 16 May 1953. Parked on the forecourt is a bus belonging to the Scottish Motor Traction Company on an extended tour down south to advertise holidays in Scotland. The semi-austerity doublc-deck Daimler bus approaching on the left is one of a batch of 100 identical vehicles delivered exclusively to Sutton Garage during 1946. It has come up the High Street and is heading for Sutton station and then onward to Epsom. *(© Alan Cross)*

Much has been said in this book and elsewhere about Sutton owing its growth to transport, firstly by the advent of the turnpike road and then by the coming of the railways. Brighton Road, formerly the London to Brighton turnpike road of which Sutton High Street is historically a part, is the latest development of a track running from the capital through Morden, Sutton and Banstead Downs to the south coast. In the mid eighteenth century the turnpike roads were huge feats of civil engineering for their day. They were usually about 60ft wide with a metalled portion in the middle for vehicles and grass borders on either side for cattle to graze as they were driven to market. Before the turnpike road, Sutton was a relatively isolated, sparsely populated, largely agricultural town. The grand new road with its toll bars and bustling traffic made a visible link with the outside world and must have added greatly, not only to the amount of employment available in the area, but also to Sutton's civic self-importance.

The London to Brighton stagecoach changed horses at Sutton. As there were up to twenty stagecoaches per day passing through, the town must have been bustling with horses, ostlers, servants of the various pubs and eateries, plus farmers and traders with goods to supply the travellers' needs. Arthur Pearson in his unpublished reminiscences of Sutton gives an example of a typical stagecoach timetable: 'In 1801 the stagecoach left the City of London at 7 a.m. and took breakfast at The Cock in Sutton at 9. Next stop was The Tangier Arms at Banstead for a glass of Miss Jeal's famous elderberry wine. Luncheon was taken at Reigate with next a two-hour stop at Stapleford Common for a famous rabbit pudding and black cherries. At Handcross they had a drop of smuggled liquor, a cup of tea at Patcham and supper at Brighton at 7p.m. [sic]' It was a twelve-hour journey.

Ninety years after the arrival of the turnpike road, on 10 May 1847, the London Brighton and South Coast Railway (LBSCR) laid the first railway tracks through Sutton. The line ran from London Bridge to Epsom via Croydon and the initial service was ten trains each way on weekdays and six on Sundays. Twenty-one years later, on 1 October 1868, the direct route to London Bridge and Victoria via Mitcham was opened and the character of the town rapidly began to change from an agricultural community to a residential area for middle-class commuters. So quickly did the town grow in the thirty years between 1851 and 1881 that the population rose tenfold from just over 1,000 to 10,334.

When the railway line to Sutton was built many of the local roads fell into disrepair as they were no longer required for the travelling public. Cars were unknown and the roads were only really used for local traffic as people who could afford to travel any distance now did so by train. The first individual form of transport available to those not absolutely wealthy were bicycles, particularly the ordinary or 'penny farthing'. It began to be manufactured in increasing numbers from about 1870 and droves of vociferous cyclists ensured that the authorities began to keep the road surface in tolerably good order.

Exactly when the first bus service came to Sutton is difficult to determine, largely because it probably started in a very ad hoc way with locals clubbing together to rent a horse-drawn carriage from a neighbour but horse-drawn buses were certainly running by the end of the nineteenth century. The first tram arrived at the Grapes terminus in Benhill Street (see p. 43) on 13 December 1906, although passengers had to wait until 21 December that year before the line was pronounced fit for passenger traffic. There was always rivalry between the two forms of transport. Horse buses usually charged more than the trams and saw themselves as catering for a slightly superior class of clientele. Trams were designed to carry a large number of people cheaply and were obliged by statute to carry workmen at reduced fares.

The first motor-bus service in the country began on 19 May 1898 in Edinburgh, but Sutton had to wait until the 1900s for its first motorised bus service and horse buses continued to be used even after motor buses were introduced. At the beginning of the twentieth century roads were often very poorly surfaced, which caused problems for early motorised road vehicles. Speaking in 1904, J.M. Birch of Birch Brothers, one of the first motor bus operators, says: 'The roads were very bad, the machines very unreliable, the drivers very inexperienced and the maintenance staff very ignorant!'

Such was the rivalry that buses and trams often served very much the same areas, occasionally to the neglect of routes seen as less profitable. For some time the area north of Sutton was very poorly served by public transport. Before the First World War Miss Mary Pochin hailed a bus on its route between Wimbledon and Sutton but the conductor was so astonished by the appearance of a customer that he totally forgot to send the requisite signal to the driver. The latter even turned to see what Miss Pochin was waving at as he drove past.

The northern end of Sutton is still the poor relation when it comes to public transport but that could change if the proposed extension to Tramlink is approved. Trams were last seen in Sutton on 7 December 1935 and in London on 5 July 1952. After a gap of almost fifty years, on 10 May 2000 Tramlink reintroduced trams to Croydon with spectacular success. If Sutton council's bid for Tramlink in the town is successful the likely route is from the railway station via Rosehill, St Helier Hospital and Mitcham to link with the Northern Line at Tooting. The plan has yet to be agreed and finance is, as always, a problem but, if agreed, Sutton might see the return of trams by 2015.

So many people now own their own car that individual transport has become self-defeating. Public transport made travel possible for ordinary people a century ago; it is doing so again today. With the proposed new tram system, six trains an hour to London and Oyster cards allowing the electronic debiting of bus fares, things have come a long way since a 1924 edition of instructions for staff issued by the Southern Railway said 'Servants of the railway must ensure that they familiarize themselves with the operation of the telephonic apparatus.'

Left: Old petrol pump, Carshalton Road, *c.* 1973. The pump was at the west end of Carshalton Road; the war memorial is just visible reflected in the window to the right of the brick column. Britain's first petrol pump appeared in Shrewsbury in 1913, although by 1921 they had spread nationwide. Before 1913 petrol, sometimes called 'motor spirit', was sold in returnable cans. Long disused, this pump still displays the price 4s 9½d. If only fuel were still this price! This site is now part of B&Q (see p. 11). *(Ron Taylor, Cheam Camera Club)*

Below: Total Garage, corner of Cheam Road and St James' Road, 7 March 2004. Self-service would have been unthinkable in the early days of motoring as only the well-to-do could have afforded cars. Garage attendants would fill cars, sometimes pumping the fuel from underground tanks by hand, take the money from the driver and return with change. The first self-service pump was installed in London in 1961. Nowadays people would be surprised to find anything else. *(George Hobbs)*

Carshalton Trolleybus Depot, Westmead Road, 31 January 1959. The sheds were opened as Sutton Tram Depot in 1906, converted to trolleybuses in 1935 and converted again to a bus garage on 3 March 1959. Its name was changed to Carshalton Trolleybus Depot – the border is roughly where the photographer is standing – to avoid confusion with the Sutton Bus Garage in Bushey Road (see p. 96). The trolleybus pictured is interesting as it is shorter than most. This type of trolleybus was used on route 654 and ran to Crystal Palace up a 1-in-9 hill. It was short to make it lighter going up and had extra brakes fitted to ensure no accidents coming down! (© A.D. Packer)

Access storage facility, 15 June 2003. Carshalton Bus Garage closed on 28 January 1964 and the buses were split between Sutton and Merton garages. The sheds were offered for sale for £13,500 but were instead leased for use as a factory. They were finally sold on 26 February 1981, although presumably the price had gone up by then. Currently Access storage solutions, the building was formerly Abacus self storage. Interestingly, although the cladding of the building is obviously new, the roof line follows the line of the old garage almost exactly. (George Hobbs)

Bushey Lane, May 1951. Sutton Bus Garage was opened on 9 January 1924 by the London General Omnibus Co. On the corner of Bushey Road and Bushey Lane it soon became bounded by the railway embankment of the Southern Railway Line linking Sutton to Wimbledon which opened on 5 January 1930; the embankment is visible in the background of the photograph. In post-war days the garage was never large enough to provide covered accommodation for the complete allocation of buses and it was common for Bushey Lane to house some of the overflow. These buses are LT single-deckers, nicknamed 'Scooters'. LT stands for 'long type' (yes really!) and they had three axles to cope with the extra weight. (© Alan Cross)

Bushey Road, 11 April 2004. Nothing changes! Despite a modern steel extension to the old brick garage, buses not in use are still parked along the road outside, the only difference being which road. Prior to the building of both bus garage and railway line the entire plot of land was used for allotments; now they are confined to one corner. The area had a tendency to be marshy and the sections of the railway line which are in a cutting still occasionally have problems with standing water. (George Hobbs)

Sutton station, *c.* 1920. As we've seen in previous pictures (see p. 43), Sutton did have trams, but not these. This is Sutton station near Jackson's Point, Ontario, and the tramcar visible is part of one of Toronto's 'radials', the local name for the interurban electric railways. There is a connection between the two Suttons. According to G.H. Armstrong, writing about the origin of place names in Canada in 1930, the village situated on Lake Simcoe in York County, Ontario, takes its name from Sutton in Surrey, England. *(Courtesy The Boston Mills Press)*

Sutton station, 26 October 2003. At street level the exterior of Sutton station has changed very little since it was built in 1928, replacing buildings dating from 1882. The station was originally a small wooden building next to the bridge on the Brighton Road. When a more substantial station was built the wooden structure was removed to Sutton Cricket Club and served as a pavilion and latterly for the scorers and groundsmen. At 10.28 on 2 February 1901 Sutton was one of the few stations to witness the passing of Queen Victoria's funeral train. Locals stood respectfully on the platform as the eight-coach train passed through the station *en route* to Victoria. *(George Hobbs)*

Left: Sutton West station, 5 July 1981, also in Ontario. The area was first known as Bourchier's Mills, after miller James O'Brien Bourchier who was appointed Georgina's first postmaster in 1831. The post office was renamed Sutton West in 1885 and the area followed suit. As in Britain there was a lot of initial opposition to the railways. One resident recalled in the *Toronto Star*: 'One man stood at his fence with a gun and dared them to go through his cornfield. They didn't do it. A widow in North Gwillimbury took her team at night and drew out the poles they had planted during the day.' Tourists soon realised the advantages of easy access, however, and Sutton West and the nearby Jackson's Point became busy with summer excursions. *(George Hobbs)*

Above: West Sutton, 26 October 2003. West Sutton station opened in early 1930 and from this angle looks very much the same now as it did then. The line was built expressly for electric trains and so the contractors, Sir Robert McAlpine & Sons, were able to build steeper inclines and sharper curves than would have been easily possible for a steam train to negotiate. The switchback severity of the line has given it the nickname 'The Wall of Death' in the railway world. *(George Hobbs)*

Right: Belmont Hospital Bridge, Good Friday, 9 April 1984. At 8 a.m. local residents were startled by an explosion when railway contractors blew up the bridge. It had been built in 1864 either as a delivery access for horse-drawn wagons to South Metropolitan District School or so that a landowner could reach the part of his ground divided by the railway line. By 1984 the school, latterly a hospital for psychiatric patients, was largely derelict and earmarked for demolition with the vacant site to be used for housing. The single-track bridge was thought to be inadequate for the expected traffic. *(George Hobbs)*

Belmont Hospital Bridge, 9 April 1984. It might have been a rude bank-holiday awakening for local residents, but Good Friday was chosen for the spectacular demolition because the Epsom Downs branch line, which runs beneath the bridge, has no service on Sundays and bank holidays. By closing the line for one day on Holy Saturday the contractors created a four-day window in which to do the necessary work. Incidentally, the photographer has not discovered the art of levitation; a temporary footbridge was erected south of the bridge parapets. (*George Hobbs*)

Belmont Hospital Bridge, 31 March 2004. On 16 November 1981 the Epsom Downs signal box burnt down, since when the service from Sutton has used only one of the two tracks. The second track was in fact lifted in 1982 giving railway enthusiasts the unusual spectacle of a single-track branch line within Greater London. The new bridge erected on the same site is a reinforced concrete structure. For twenty years it has covered the full width of the two-line trackbed just in case the second line is reinstated. Terrorism has meant that explosions in peacetime are regrettably becoming more common. Even so some locals still call this the 'Boom Bridge'! (*George Hobbs*)

5

The Things People Do . . .

Protest rally outside Quadrant House, 22 February 1993. The rally was organised by the Graphical, Paper & Media Union (GPMU) outside the UK premises of Reed Business Information, one of the UK's leading magazine publishers. In 1986 News International had introduced new technology which made it possible to produce mass-circulation newspapers without using skilled print workers. In 1993 the same organisation started a price war by cutting cover prices and increasing circulation of their titles at the expense of others. Reed and other publishing conglomerates followed suit often to the detriment of print workers in smaller publishers. The GPMU's protest was supported by representatives from various other unions. Notable speakers included John Smith, leader of the Labour Party until his death on 12 May 1994. *(Ron Taylor, Cheam Camera Club)*

Regardless of the buildings, roads or transport which exist in the area, a community is essentially a collection of people. Tantalising glimpses of Sutton residents appear in old records or as monuments in the parish church. One such, at the west end of the south aisle of St Nicholas', is a small white marble monument to Isaac Littlebury, traveller and linguist, who died 30 April 1710, aged 53. He was the son of a Covent Garden bookseller, could speak French, Latin and Italian and translated many of the classics, but no details are known of his life in Sutton. Was he a private tutor to one of the large families? Had he retired to the country for his health or so that he could work on some translation in peace? Or was he the eighteenth-century equivalent of Bill Bryson, travelling around the country collecting material for a book, who happened to die on his journey?

In communities relatively isolated from the outside world, people had to look after their own. Times were harder, but even so certain standards of behaviour were expected and it was unwise to do too much to upset the neighbours. The part of Surrey into which Sutton fell had a local 'cure' for a man who was known to beat his wife. Locals would lay a train of chaff to his cottage door indicating that they knew that thrashing was taking place. If the husband didn't take the hint neighbours would surround the dwelling and beat kettles and pans causing a din which advertised his actions.

Self-reliance was still apparent in the Sutton community at the beginning of the twentieth century. Rather like the lifeboat crews around Britain's coast today, the town relied on volunteers to provide its fire brigade. The horse-drawn engine was stationed in the High Street (see p. 42) and depended on animals from the council dust carts for its motive power. Warning of fires and a call for the crew and horses to muster was made by a steam-driven hooter on the roof of Dendy Napper's flour mill at 86 High Street; the premises originally housed the police station.

Dendy Napper was one of the characters of Sutton and locals still know the name. His flour mill and bakery was reputed to be one of the largest in the UK with an extensive shop frontage on the High Street. Dendy Napper came to Sutton in the late 1860s having been born in Pyrford in about 1848. He was a warden of St Nicholas' Church, a freemason and founder of the Sutton Lodge, an enthusiastic sportsman and a member of the Sutton Local Board of Health. This last meant that he was concerned with the arrangement of street cleaning, refuse collection, drainage and sanitation before the council began organising such services centrally. Dendy Napper died in 1909 but his bakery business was continued in his name for some years.

William Roberti, President of a huge North American clothing group, said, 'The customer is the most important person in any retail environment.' The Sutton Town Centre Traders' Association would certainly agree. Every summer it organises various events to keep shoppers entertained. The live music performed in the Millennium Gardens by local bands and musicians on Saturdays and Thursday evenings, the puppet festival, the French markets and the craft fairs that take place in the pedestrianised section of the High Street are all courtesy of the Traders' Association. Not only William Roberti but also Dendy Napper would have approved.

The fact that local residents do their best to look after each other becomes even more obvious looking down the list of benefactions given to the parish. Most are to benefit the poor and educate their children, but one or two reveal a practical common sense in keeping with those who live on the land. Elizabeth Stephens, for example, gave £200 – a considerable sum in 1782 when the bequest was made – for cleaning and beautifying the church and making good the footpaths of the parish. The community at the time lived only on moisture-bearing Thanet sand (see introduction to Chapter 1), so the footpaths may well have been muddy and impassable in places.

One legacy which benefited the community is something of a mystery. The Gibson tomb in St Nicholas' churchyard was erected by Mary Gibson in 1777. By her will, dated 1793, she also left a sum of money for the parish officers and poor (see p. 54) providing that the vault is kept in good repair and inspected every year on 12 August. Dr George Williamson, writing in 1924, adds: 'It is believed in the Gibson family that when the last member of the family has been buried in the vault, it is finally to be locked, the key taken to Palestine and thrown into the river Jordan.' As the family seems to have no connection with Sutton apart from its tomb it would be difficult to track down the last family member. Even so the tradition, unbroken for over two hundred years, is to cease from 2004. Shame.

The common understanding of shared work was often the backbone of much community fellowship and large organisations often had their own social clubs. Sutton District Water Company's Athletic and Social Club was formed in 1928 and its football team in particular has been very successful. The Institute of Cancer Research (ICR) is another local organisation whose employees play as well as work together. ICR staff not only enjoy social events such as quiz evenings and an annual Mini-Olympics, but also field teams to raise money for charity. Staff teams have run in the London Marathon, various fun runs and, most gruelling of all, a 150-mile run across the Sahara desert. Many of the staff participate in one sport or another but ICR's Allan Thornhill is a bit special. He was bowled over to be offered the chance to umpire at the Commonwealth Games in July 2002. His sport? Lawn bowls.

How the town entertains itself has changed over the years, but entertain itself it certainly has. From the end of the eighteenth century to the beginning of the twenty-first the town's community has known how to have fun. Entertainment may have changed from pageantry to parks, and from dance halls to dance classes, but Sutton still has a lot going on for residents and visitors alike to enjoy. After a year which saw two general elections one famous photograph from 1910 shows Sutton High Street decorated for Christmas Show Week with a banner which says 'HANG POLITICS LET'S BE JOLLY'. I'll vote for that.

The start of the half-marathon, 23 March 1986. Sutton's third half-marathon was sponsored by 'Times 2', which manages one of Sutton's shopping malls. The marathon started in Collingwood recreation ground and finished in Sutton United football ground. Even though part of the route was up the High Street – 1 in 9 at the top – over 1,000 competitors completed the course. The first three home are all visible in the front row in this picture. Second from the left, wearing 1749, is N. Boyle who came second. D. Wright, wearing 1053 and fifth from the left, won the event in 1 hour, 10 minutes and 7 seconds. Third placed was D. Faircott, far right wearing 1114. Proceeds from the half-marathon went to Radio Lollipop's appeal for a new home for long-stay patients at Queen Mary's Hospital for Children at Carshalton. *(Ron Taylor, Cheam Camera Club)*

In 1950, was this the smallest television receiver in the world? Claimed by the local paper to be vest-pocket size (waistcoat pockets must have been bigger then) the mini-television set was nevertheless a staggering achievement for its time. Measuring $10 \times 7 \times 4$in it showed television programmes on the tiny screen, visible as the white square above the set of knobs. It could also double as a radio and provided the light or home service programmes merely by flicking a switch. A member of Sutton and Cheam Radio Society, Lawrence White, its designer/builder, was only 17. (*Courtesy of Sutton and Cheam Radio Society*)

Opposite, above: Sutton Adult School exhibition, 1950. Before the 1953 coronation, when the pageantry showed what television could do, sets were few and far between. The Sutton and Cheam Radio Society staged an exhibition of new technology at the Sutton Adult School Hall and included a 12in set made by one of the members. The *Sutton and Cheam Herald* claimed that it 'incorporated many features not yet to be found in commercial receivers'. The hall was packed with people interested in seeing this technological wonder. Behind the television, left to right: Stan Vanstone (G2AYC), Roderick Clews (G3CDK) and two other members who can no longer be identified. (*Courtesy of Sutton and Cheam Radio Society*)

Opposite, below: Modern amateur radio equipment belonging to members of Sutton & Cheam Radio Society, 14 November 2003. On the left is an Icom IC-756PRO short-wave amateur radio transceiver which has a full-colour multi-functional display and is capable of making contact with other radio amateurs anywhere in the world. On the right is a Yaesu VX-1 low power VHF/UHF handheld transceiver. Note the size in comparison with a 9-v battery; unlike the 1950 mini-television, the transceiver really is capable of being carried in a shirt pocket. Line-of-sight communication over a few miles is possible using this type of equipment, but the incorporated receiver also allows reception of broadcast VHF FM radio transmissions together with the sound transmissions from local television stations. Similar equipment has been used to receive signals from radio amateurs who are astronauts on the International Space Station. (*George Hobbs*)

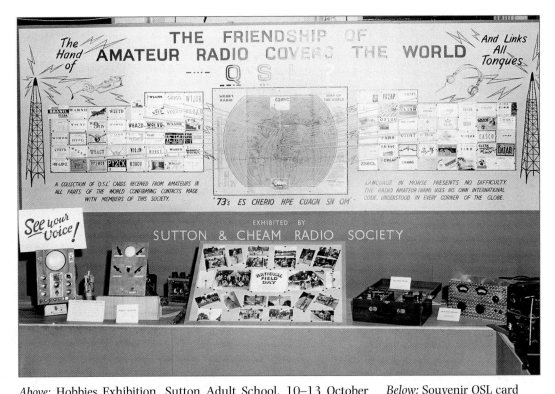

Above: Hobbies Exhibition, Sutton Adult School, 10–13 October 1951. Amateur radio operators each have a unique call sign with which to identify themselves on air. The letter at the beginning of the call sign indicates the country in which the operator is licensed; British call signs, for example, begin with G or M. The ability to send and receive Morse is no longer a requirement for an amateur licence, but many still use this mode of transmission. However even speedy operators find tapping out each character time consuming. Radio hams consequently developed a kind of shorthand. The message '73s ES CHERIO HPE CUAGN SN OM' below the central map means 'Best wishes and cheerio; hope to see you again soon old man'. Amateur radio enthusiasts have been text-messaging for more than half a century. *(Courtesy of Sutton and Cheam Radio Society)*

Below: Souvenir QSL card from Hobbies Exhibition, 10–13 October 1951. G4DH/A was the temporary call sign for the exhibition station, creating by adding suffix /A to G4DH which was the call sign for club member G.R. Pearson. The suffix indicated that he was not operating from his home address. In amateur radio circles Q codes are used for brevity and clarity in routine communication. QSO means 'contact', while QSL means 'I acknowledge receipt of transmission'; QSL cards are exchanged as a courtesy and confirmation of two-way communication with another 'ham'. The display above shows the collection of QSL cards received by the society from places as far away as South America and the Far East. This card is just visible at the bottom of the central map. *(Courtesy of Sutton and Cheam Radio Society)*

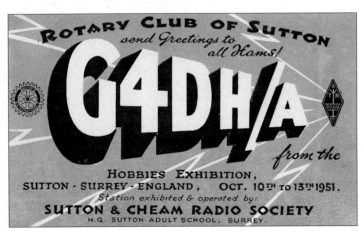

Boys from Homefield Preparatory School transmitting on air, *c.* 1950. This stand was organised by the Sutton and Cheam Radio Society at one of the various exhibitions the members attended with their equipment. In the 1950s there was no National Curriculum, of course, but nowadays pupils are required to study information and communications technology and create and build their own products. Building an AM radio is a recognised way of fulfilling many of the criteria for Key Stage 3. Key Stage 3 pupils are generally between 11 and 14, so a little older than those in the picture, and the equipment is a little more sophisticated, with printed circuit boards rather than valves, but the principle hasn't changed much in fifty years. *(Courtesy of Sutton and Cheam Radio Society)*

3rd Sutton Boys' Brigade in gaol! Around Christmas 1987 PC Nick Cornish arranged for boys from the brigade to visit Sutton police station. Among other things, the boys saw the operations centre, explored a police car and felt what it was like to be behind bars (they seem remarkably cheerful about it!). Sutton Independent Custody Visitors (SICV) regularly make unannounced visits to the police station to check on the welfare of people in police custody. Their aim is to reassure the local community that detainees are treated appropriately. Certainly the boys' brigade seem to have no complaints. *(Ron Taylor, Cheam Camera Club)*

Sydney Bottle Club outing, 1913. The club surrounds a charabanc outside the Sydney Public House on the corner of Sydney Road and Collingwood Road. Looking out of the upstairs window is Mrs Turnbull, wife of the licensee (no. 49 in list below). Pictured are: 1, Harry Hook, park keeper; 2, ? Nichols, boot and shoe repairer; 3, Harry Walden, painter; 4, ? Barton; 5, Len Muggeridge; 6, Charlie Prior, Brocks Firework technician; 7, ? Earl; 8, Len Cooper, painter; 9, ? Francis, council worker; 10, 'Buster' West; 11, G. Reid; 12, ? Larkin, postman and nurseryman; 13, 'Bunny' Burton; 14, J. Martin, Gas Co. employee; 15, ? Burtenshaw; 16, Joe Cope, fishmonger; 17, G. Palmer, blacksmith; 18, Harry Card, telephone wireman; 19, M. Spalding, verger of The Good Shepherd; 20, Bill Martin; 21, Tom Hook, Gas Co. employee; 22, M. Dalton; 23, ? Tichener, scrap metal merchant; 24, Walter Wood, greengrocer;

25, ? Hunt, scrap metal merchant; 26, Sam Glover; 27, J. Timson; 28, ? Austin; 29, ? Harvey; 30, A. Kent Jnr.; 31, ? Franklyn; 32, -?-; 33, ? Napper; 34, G. Austin, painter; 35, 'Darkie' Histed; 36, Harry Keel, carpenter; 37, Polly Martin; 38, Mrs Napper; 39, C. Napper; 40, Alf Radley, telephone wireman; 41, Bert Bryant; 42, 'Teddy' Waldon, painter; 43, Phil Yeoman, council worker; 44, Jack Maynard; 45, Fred Prior, chauffeur; 46, ? Mapstone, could play almost any musical instrument; 47, ? Wing, property owner, who bought most of the houses in Sydney Road for £25 each (see p. 50); 48, ? Stimpson, brick maker; 49, ? Turnbull, licensee of the Sydney public house; 50, ? Stevens Snr., wheelwright; 51, ? Stevens, hod carrier; 52, ? Elsey, painter; 53, ? Tearle, meat porter; 54, ? Kent; 55, Charles Prior; 56, 'Sonny' King; 57, Ted Stevens. (*Courtesy Pearson Cycle Specialists*)

Sutton District Water Company outing, 26 July 1919. Social events have always been a part of the Water Company's tradition. Here staff enjoy a day trip to Brighton. Back row, left to right: D. Windsor, Jim Quick, W. Millson, -?-, P. Bignall, Jack Quick (brother of Jim). Third row: R. Brewster, A. Peters, 'Old Joe' Gregory, W. Blackmore, 'Fatty' Knowler, C. Windsor, -?-. Second row: Bob Brewster (son of R. Brewster), Bill Elliott, W. Hooper, G. Fairs, H. Kenyon, F. Phillips, P. Walker, G. Hills, G. Friend. First row: W. Mercer, T. Kavanagh, Cooper Elliott (Bill's father), A. Wilde. The ladies in the background are not named. *(Courtesy of Sutton and East Surrey Water)*

Sutton District Water Company v. Sutton Council rounders match, 1987. Rounders has been played since the eighteenth century where it is synonymous with baseball; over the decades the two versions divided to develop along parallel lines. Rounders is generally considered the quieter and less commercial of the two sports so why Caroline Strutt of the water company is threatening Howard Spencer of the council is not clear. Perhaps the council won! *(Courtesy of Sutton and East Surrey Water)*

Waverley Avenue, 16 October 1987. On the night of 15 October 7,000 trees fell in the area's streets, 2,000 of them blocking roads. The wind was known to be gusting in excess of 100mph, and some meteorologists suggest that the funnel effect of the streets could have made it much more. Battered buildings, scattered debris and squashed cars were common in the changed landscape. All credit to the owner of this one for having a sense of humour! *(Sue Poulter)*

Waverley Avenue, looking east, 15 June 2003. The road has a sharp bend at its east end as it was built to follow the original field boundaries. At the bend was an old pond and orchard and the back gardens of this section of the road originally contained one or more of the old apple trees. Waverley Avenue is built on part of what was Woodend Garden Suburb, one of about twenty similar garden suburb developments built around the country in the decade before the First World War. *(George Hobbs)*

Left: King's Lane overbridge, looking west, 16 October 1987. This is the main line from Sutton to Victoria going through Carshalton, Hackbridge and Mitcham Junction. There seems to be a problem with leaves on the line. Sutton (usually) has an extremely good train service, which is one of the reasons it has become an important business centre. No commuters got to work by train on this day, however. Ironically, Victoria was the only London railway station to remain open. (*George Hobbs*)

Right: King's Lane overbridge, looking west, 21 December 2003. A 455 electric suburban unit heads under the bridge towards Carshalton and London. Just in front of the train the third rail swaps from one side of the track to the other. The third rail is held in place by its own weight and not fixed. Being steel it expands and contracts according to the weather. Swapping the rail from one side of the track to the other keeps the rail lengths short and therefore minimises distortion as the rail heats and cools. (*George Hobbs*)

Homefield Preparatory School, Western Road, October 1987. Sutton had a large number of mature trees and was particularly severely hit by the hurricane. Fortunately most of the damage occurred to property rather than people, because the worst of the weather occurred at night when fewer people were about. Some creatures didn't seem to mind too much. To the west of Sutton one old tree housed a bees' nest in its trunk. When the tree fell the bees didn't seem to mind that their home had been rotated through 90° and remained throughout the winter. *(Ron Taylor, Cheam Camera Club)*

Homefield Preparatory School, Western Road, 21 February 2004. Founded in 1870, the school became a charitable trust in 1967 when the previous owner sold the land and the school moved to its present location. It caters for around 380 boys aged 2–14. The school has experienced significant expansion and restructuring since 1967, the most obvious being the new reception area. *(George Hobbs)*

Chris Pearson, 1934. The uncle of the present owners of Pearson Cycle Specialists (see p. 39), Chris was a farmer for many years. He appears to be wearing a copy of the mayoral robes and be about to take part in a procession. On 12 September 1934 Sutton and Cheam received the charter promoting it from an urban district to a borough. A lengthy procession wound through the streets to celebrate the event and was largely made up of floats supplied by the town's traders. Could Chris be taking part? (*Courtesy Pearson Cycle Specialists*)

Town centre cycle race, 11 June 2000. The riders have cycled up the High Street and are just about to turn left into Throwley Road before riding down Throwley Way to complete the circuit. Typically a race of this sort would last an hour or be for a certain number of laps. Such a race obviously requires police permission, particularly in this case where a road needed to be closed. The British Cycling Federation is the governing body for all road-racing events, which are ridden under federation rules and covered by its insurance. Wearing the Pearson strip, one of the local boys leads the pack. (*George Hobbs*)

6

Sutton as it Might Have Been

NORTH ELEVATION

Design for the rectory for St Nicholas' Church, 1887. This architect's drawing is of the rectory which was actually built, but there were two other designs which never left the drawing board. Pictured is the front of the rectory whose entrance was at the end of a long drive from West Street. The window to the right of the front door was that of a waiting room which led directly into the study, the bay window of which can just be seen on the far right. On the far left are two small doors, the one with two windows to a coal house and the other marked as the tradesmen's entrance. Half of the window next to it belonged to the larder, while the other half gave light onto a passageway and caused someone to write the scribbled comment: 'Useless window giving onto an unused space. Alone it would be bricked up.' On the first floor, the single window on the left is for the day nursery; the night nursery was next door to the left, with its window facing south (see p. 32). (Courtesy St Nicholas' Church)

Fiction has no place in a book of photographs showing Sutton past and present, but in any town there will have been ideas for development, change and possibly improvement that were never acted upon. Sutton has seen many proposals suggested, even promoted over the years, but which for one reason or another never happened.

Some of the possible developments for Sutton go back a long way. Up until the middle of the fifteenth century Sutton Manor was owned by Chertsey Abbey which had the right to appoint the rector of the parish, collect rent from its lands, etc. Some time before the fifteenth century the Abbot of Chertsey granted the Lord of the Manor of Sutton the right to erect a gallows, a pillory and a cucking stool. A ducking stool was a chair at the end of a see-saw in which the person to be punished wass ducked in a river or pond. Some authorities suggest that a cucking stool was a chair in which the wrongdoer was fastened and then suspended by means of a pulley. As well as being able to throw objects and insults, onlookers also had the fun of swinging and spinning the unfortunate victim. An aerial form of stocks, if that's what a cucking stool was, might be a more appropriate explanation for an area where water was not particularly abundant. The gallows and the pillory were certainly built because there are reports of them being used, but there is no record of anyone being sentenced to a spell in the cucking stool. They surely would not have gone to the trouble of building one if it remained unused.

The idea of turning what was a chalk pit in Carshalton Road and is now the site of B&Q into pleasure gardens has already been mentioned on p. 12. What has not been emphasised is how the plans had taken definite shape. The *Sutton and Epsom Advertiser* of 31 May 1907 said: 'among its umbrageous foliage shady walks could be made, little niches for seats provided and charming effects would be produced, especially if the miniature lake at the bottom could be perpetuated.' *The Herald* for 1 June 1907 agreed and suggested that the chalk pit 'is so picturesque that at very little expense it might be converted into a pleasure ground. The construction of a few paths and the planting of a few shrubs here and there would meet all the requirements . . . With pleasant walks, a bowling green or two and a band stand or enclosure in which one or other of the town bands could discourse sweet music. . . . would do something to relieve the town from the reproach of being dull.' It seems a far cry from B&Q.

We've already seen that Sutton was the most westerly terminus of the South Metropolitan Electric Tramways (see p. 43). Sutton had a good tramcar service to Croydon about 6 miles to the east, but nothing at all to Mitcham, about 4 miles to the north. Very unusually, no tram line was constructed on the main road north to London and it seems that Croydon was considered by the locals a more important centre than the metropolis. The strange gap is particularly apparent looking at service maps of the time where routes were highlighted. There seems no apparent geo-graphical reason why a tram route was not built as there were no steep hills which a tram could not negotiate easily. Mitcham was at that time a growing centre of popula-tion and even if it had not been such a consideration did not usually weigh heavily with tram and train companies, which knew that suburban housing would develop around the access routes. So odd is the omission that the current Tramlink proposal for a tram route in Sutton (see introduction to Chapter 4) has ignored other possibilities and focused on recommending the installation of the exact line which was omitted so many years ago.

The closest underground connection to Sutton is with the Northern Line at Morden, but if the First World War had not intervened Sutton could have had its own connection with the District Line. In 1910 an Act of Parliament was passed granting permission for the construction of a 5½-mile railway line between Wimbledon and Sutton and approval given for it to be run by the Metropolitan District Railway. Minor work was started at Wimbledon in 1913, and by 1914 the land for the Sutton line was purchased and fenced.

The route was planned to take in the current Wimbledon Chase, South Merton and Morden South stations, although they were to be called Cannon Hill, Merton Park and Morden respectively. Sutton Common and West Sutton stations were also planned for roughly where they are now, although the latter was to be called Collingwood Road. There was, however, to be an additional station called Cheam. It was to be situated on the north side of Cheam Road near Western Road. The proposed Sutton terminus of this end of the District line was to be either side of Bridge Road with its booking office located 150 yards west of the High Street.

The plan was proposed and costed quite carefully and would almost certainly have gone ahead if the First World War had not intervened. The rising cost of building, both of the railway itself and houses for the passengers who would use it, delayed its construction until the route was taken over by the Southern Railway. Sutton ended up with a circuitous overland route of relatively few trains and tortuous connections, as opposed to an alternative fast and through service to central London.

If the First World War was responsible for killing off the proposed District Line connection, the Second World War put paid to a much more extreme proposal made by Sir Charles Bressey and Sir Edwin Lutyens. Their 1938 *Highway Development Survey for Greater London* proposed an overhead high-level road with four lanes of traffic joining the Barnet bypass with Croydon. One proposed route for the new road, although admittedly not the most favoured, took it through north Sutton.

More recently, in the 1970s when Sutton Council were considering options for the new ring road, plans were put forward to create a pedestrian underpass at The Cock to allow traffic to pass unimpeded along Cheam Road and Carshalton Road. Nothing came of the idea and traffic and pedestrians still converge at the old crossroads. More recently still, in 1984, J. Sainsbury went to the lengths of commissioning Eric Davies to prepare a photographic volume illustrating the extent, character and premises of the then disused Sutton waterworks as the possible site for a store. The proposal came to nothing and the Water Gardens estate was built instead.

We can all postulate 'what ifs' and imagine Sutton still with its Manor House and trolley buses or without a pedestrianised High Street, but this chapter gives a taste of some definite plans which were shelved. As the story books say: 'Once upon a time . . .'.

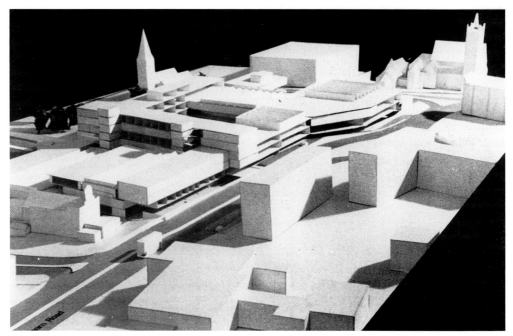

Model of Sutton, planned layout looking east, *c.* 1970. In the top right corner is Trinity Methodist Church, top left is St Nicholas' and bottom left what is now the Secombe Theatre. The civic centre was to be bounded by what is now St Nicholas Way and the Secombe Theatre east and west. It was to be built in three phases. Phase 1 containing the council chamber, mayor's offices and committee rooms, arts college, library and assembly rooms was to be completed by April 1974. Phase 2 containing civic offices was scheduled for completion in 1976 and phase 3 comprising more civic offices and car parking should have been completed by 1978. In fact phase 3, the low block of buildings nearest the Secombe Theatre, was never built and changes to the planned accommodation became inevitable. *(Author's collection)*

Cheam Road, looking east, 11 April 2004. The Secombe Theatre is on the left of the picture, but beyond it, where phase 3 of the civic centre was to have been built, is the Holiday Inn and car park. The hotel is one of the most modern in the town with air-conditioning and modem points in the bedrooms and indoor pool, gym, sauna and video-conferencing facilities. Perhaps the sale of the site helped to fund the new civic offices? *(George Hobbs)*

Model of Sutton planned layout looking north, *c.* 1970. Trinity Methodist Church is in the bottom right corner while on the other side of the triangular road junction is Sutton Baptist Church. Such a large new complex would obviously have a similarly large impact on the environment. The proposals suggested that a low-rise building would fit in better with the scale of the churches and other buildings surrounding the site and added that 'particular attention will be given to the landscape treatment'. Phase 3, the furthest west part of the civic centre and that closest to the Secombe Theatre, was never built. It was to house the Borough Engineer and Surveyor's Department and the Department of Architecture and Planning. *(Author's collection)*

Civic centre, looking north-west, 11 April 2004. On the left Sutton Baptist Church is just visible with the Holiday Inn in the distance beyond. Although a low-rise building on the same site, the building which was erected bears very little resemblance to that proposed. The two blocks are more uniform, the windows more prominent and the road straight rather than detouring round the centre. *(George Hobbs)*

Right: Model of the Catholic Church of Our Lady of the Rosary, 1913. John Hawes, as well as designing the chancel extension (see p. 65), was asked to design a bell tower intended to rise 70ft above the ground. Two versions of the design exist, the one modelled plus a water colour painting dated August 1913 detailing the tower shown in the front of the photograph with an additional and very small spire surmounted by a cross on top. No record has yet come to light about why the bell tower was not built as intended, but the onset of the First World War may well have been a contributing factor. *(Courtesy of the Church of Our Lady of the Rosary)*

Below: Catholic Church of Our Lady of the Rosary, 21 December 2003. This is the corner of Bramley Road and St Barnabas' Road. It appears from this view of the north-west corner of the church that the lower part of the bell tower was indeed built – it was never built to its full intended height – possibly at the same time as the north aisle whose windows are visible to the left. Bramley Road, in which the white car is parked, was laid out in 1911 on land owned by Thomas Berney. He lived in Clifton House, Bramley Hill, Croydon, which is how the road gets its name. *(George Hobbs)*

Design for a new organ, St Nicholas' church, *c.* 1887. At the same time as designing a new rectory (see p. 32), architect E.J. Perrott also gave some thought to the installation of a new organ in the church. Just indicated in the centre of the picture is the memorial to Dorothy, Lady Brownlowe, daughter of Sir Richard Mason one time Lord of the Manor of Sutton. Lady Brownlowe died in 1700 and the memorial was originally erected in the old church (see p. 2). When the church was demolished in 1864 the memorial was moved to the north aisle of the current church. It stretches nearly as high as the ceiling and still exists although it is totally concealed by the organ. *(Courtesy St Nicholas' Church)*

Organ, St Nicholas' church, 31 March 2004. The organ was constructed in 1899 by the Norwich organ builders, Norman and Beard. The firm began in the 1870s as Norman Bros, organ tuners. In the 1880s the two brothers were joined by G. Wales Beard and established a workshop in Norwich. By the turn of the century they had been responsible for building instruments all over East Anglia and went on to build organs as far afield as Johannesburg. In 1916 the firm was taken over by William Hill & Sons and now trades as Hill, Norman and Beard. *(George Hobbs)*

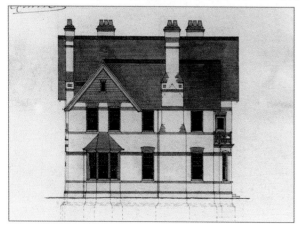

Designs for the rectory for
St Nicholas' Church, 1887. The top
four pictures, showing two designs
each from the north and south
sides, were never built. The lower
two pictures show the west and east
elevation of the rectory actually
built (see also p. 32 and 117). The
small door faced east and was the
tradesmen's entrance, while the bay
window facing the pleasant gardens
to the west was that of the rector's
study. Note the number of
chimneys: exactly how many were
intended? Or is there some artistic

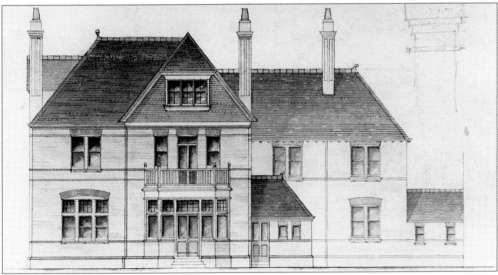

licence even in the architects' plans? Incidentally, one of the architects, E.T. Perrott, was living at 16 High Street at the time, so probably had a vested interest in what was built relatively close to home. His colleague R.L. Cole lived in Cavendish Road and so was probably less personally concerned. Interestingly the plans for the rectory were approved by the surveyor for the Diocese of Rochester; St Nicholas' church is now in the Diocese of Southwark. *(Courtesy St Nicholas' Church)*

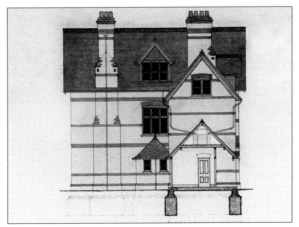

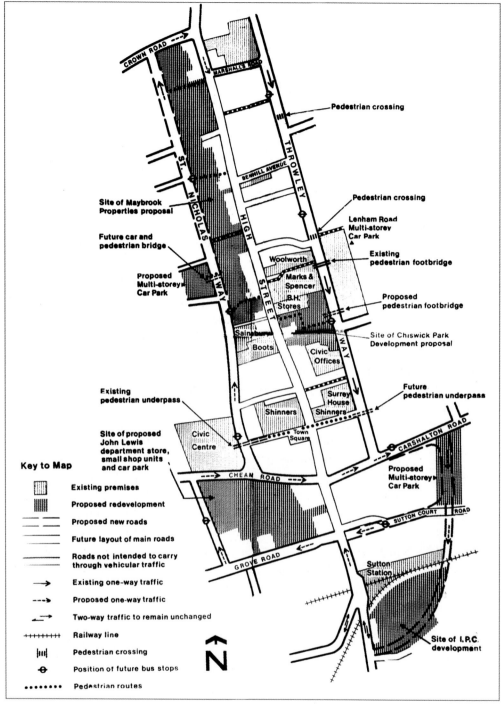

Proposed plan of Sutton town centre, spring 1978. Many of the details are different but there are also major proposals which never materialised. Neither the proposed new road around the back of Sutton station and linking Carshalton Road with Brighton Road nor the John Lewis department store was ever built. In its leaflet advocating the early exclusion of traffic from the High Street the council says that 'bus stops will be sited on the inside of the parallel roads (St Nicholas Way and Throwley Way) . . . it will not be necessary to cross the increasingly busy parallel roads.' Something else that didn't happen, then. . . . *(Author's collection)*

ACKNOWLEDGEMENTS

Without the support, suggestions, help and photographic skills of my husband, George Hobbs, this book would not have been possible. Every effort has been made to locate all the copyright holders and obtain their permission to use the photographic material included in this book. If there has been any error or omission in crediting the correct individuals or organisations the author can only apologise.

I am indebted to many organisations for their willingness to help with photographic material for this book. They include: All Saints' Benhilton Church of England Primary School; the Church of Our Lady of the Rosary; Georgina Public Libraries, Ontario; Pearson Cycle Specialists; Overton Grange School; Robin Hood Infants School; Robin Hood Junior School; The Religious Society of Friends; St Nicholas' Church; Sutton and Cheam Radio Society (www.scrs.org.uk); Sutton and East Surrey Water Company Ltd; Sutton Grammar School; Sutton High School; Sutton Jewish Community.

I should also like to thank the many individuals who rootled through their own or neighbour's lofts and cheerfully gave up their time to provide help, information and cups of tea. Many of them also allowed their photographs and other material to be reproduced. They include: Karen Baker, Mary Baxter (Branch Librarian, Peter Gzowski Branch Library, Ontario), A.P.W. Collins, Pauline Cook, Alan Cross, Ann Dent, Gary Drostle, Emma Hart Dyke, the Revd Sara Goatcher, Margaret Holland, Gill Hutton, Gordon Ironside, Sue James, June Lewis, Dr Peter Likeman, Fr Jim McGillicuddy, Mary Morris, Kieran Osborne, A.D. Packer, Denise Parrett, Guy Pearson, William Pearson, Derek and Sue Poulter, John Puttock, Lesley Pynor, Gordon and Pat Steel, Maureen Swains, Ron Taylor, Stephen and Sue Waters.

BIBLIOGRAPHY

Much of the information for the captions in this book has been provided by the people who have loaned the photographs, but some has, of necessity, been derived from other documentation. The author acknowledges with gratitude the debt she owes to the following:

Andrew, Martin. *Around Sutton*, Frith Book Co., 2001

Anon. *The Sutton District Water Company 1863–1963*, Sutton and Cheam Water Company Ltd, 1963.

Burgess, Frank. *Sutton, A Pictorial History*, Phillimore, 1993

Heater, Derek, *Keeping Faith: a History of Sutton Grammar School*, Sutton Grammar School, 1999

Jones, A.E. *A Small School in the Great War*, A.E. Jones, 1975

Jones, Jane E.M. *Images of England: Sutton*, Tempus, 1998

Lewis, June (ed.). *ALON*, Sutton Jewish Community magazine

Marshall, C.J. *History of Cheam and Sutton*, Cryer's Library, 1936

Mitchell, Vic and Smith, Keith. *London Suburban Railways: West Croydon to Epsom*, Middleton Press, 1992

Nairn, Ian and Pevsner, Nikolaus. *The Buildings of England: Surrey*, second edition, Penguin Books Ltd, 1971

Pearson, Arthur. *Old Sutton*, unpublished reminiscences, 1974

Stamp, Robert M. *Riding the Radials*, The Boston Mills Press, 1989

Steel, G. Gordon. *An Outline History of Sutton Meeting, 1932–2000*, Sutton Preparatory Meeting, 2001

Various. *The London Railway Record*, no. 24, Conner & Butler, 2000

Williamson, Dr George C. *Curious Survivals*, Parkgate Books, 1997